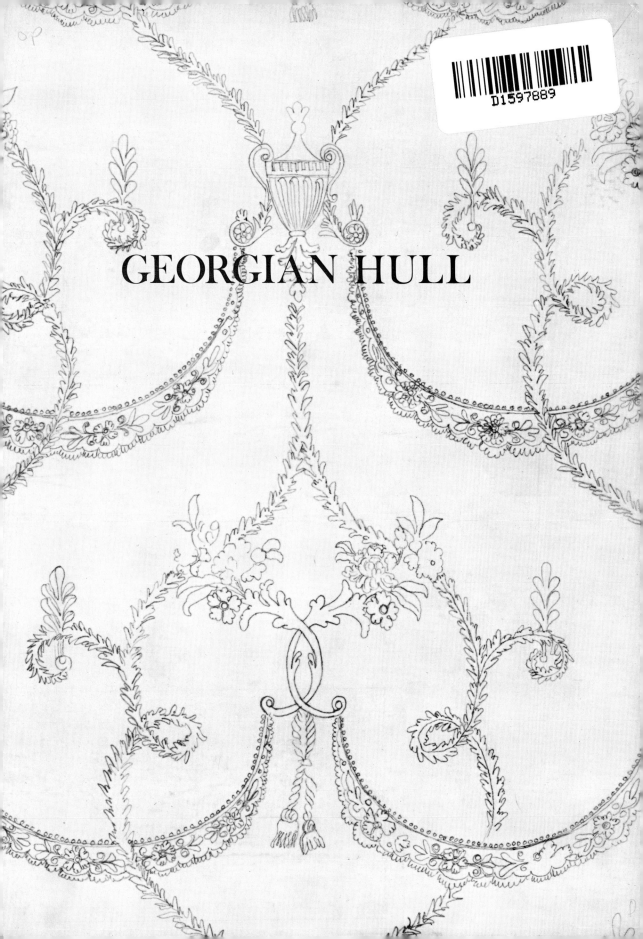

GEORGIAN HULL

A NEW PICTURE OF

GEORGIAN

HULL

To Fritz and Lieselotte.

Written and Illustrated by

Ivan and Elisabeth Hall

William Sessions Limited
York, England
in association with
Hull Civic Society

This book has been sponsored by Hull Civic Society, who wish to acknowledge the generous help given by the following Trusts: Colonel and Mrs. Rupert Alec-Smith's Charitable Settlements, The Plaut Charitable Trust and The Marc Fitch Fund.

ISBN 0 900657 43 X

© I. and E. A. F. Hall

Phototypeset in 10/11 point Times and printed by William Sessions Ltd., The Ebor Press, York, England. Platemaking by City Engraving Co. (Hull) Ltd.

FOR RUPERT AND SUZETTE

First published 1978/9

ACKNOWLEDGEMENTS

This book could not have been written without the warm help and encouragement of Colonel Rupert A. Alec-Smith, and we are much indebted to his intimate knowledge of Hull's architecture and of the families for whom the buildings were created. We are also much indebted to the Chief Officers of the City of Kingston-upon-Hull: the Town Clerk and Chief Executive, the Chief Planning Officer, the Director of Industrial Development and his staff, Mr. John Bradshaw and his staff, for help generously given. We should similarly like to express our gratitude to Mr. G. Oxley and Mrs. H. Allison for bringing additional material to our notice. We are also equally indebted to Mr. K. Holt and Mr. C. N. Snowden and Mrs. C. Boddington of the Humberside County Record Office; and to Miss J. Crowther and Mr. G. P. Brown of Humberside County Council Libraries for their kindness over a prolonged period. Dr. Gordon Drummond has again helped us with the memorials in the Land Registry, as did Mrs. Lesley Woledge. We are also most grateful to the Board of Trinity House and their staff for their generous help in our research into the architectural development of the House. Their surveyor Mr. J. Barling kindly introduced us to much important new material. Mr. R. Reid is gratefully thanked for his help with the techniques of wood carving. We owe a special debt to Messrs. Broady, Messrs. Sam Allon and Messrs. Thompson, for their help in allowing us to record buildings and salvage fragments from the sites entrusted to them. Without their co-operation much useful knowledge would have been lost. Mr. B. Ayres, Mrs. Ball, Messrs. Blackmore & Son, the Rev. C. B. Bridgeman, Mr. A. Bray, Messrs. Boots (Whitefriargate Branch); Mr. A. G. Chamberlain, Mr. and Mrs. J. Chichester-Constable, Mr. I. A. Cooper, the Rev. and Mrs. Norman Dunning, Dr. Terry Friedman, Mr. B. Foster, Mr. N. Higson, Mr. Huntsman, Mr. Francis Johnson, Mr. I. A. Johnson, Mr. P. Martin, Mr. & Mrs. D. Neave, Mr. A. Royle, Mr. D. Scarrott, Mrs. G. Spencer, Miss L. Stead and the United Towing Company have all helped us and shared information. We must also thank the many owners who have allowed us to study and to photograph their homes and offices, and thanks are also due to William Sessions Ltd., and in particular to Mr. J. B. Blackwell for planning this book for press with his characteristic good humoured patience.

The under-mentioned have kindly allowed us to take the following photographs:–
Humberside County Council, *figs. 175, 188, 189*. The City of Kingston-upon-Hull, *figs. 2, 18, 76, 77, 79, 187, 213-16, 218, 257, 268*. Trinity House, *figs. 134, 139-42, 144-47, 151-53, 156-60, 162-64*. Birmingham City Reference Library, *fig. 245*. Castle Museum, York, *figs. 129, 130, 131, 133*. Mr. A. G. Chamberlain, *fig. 246*. Mr. I. Ashley Cooper, *fig. 48*. Messrs Gelder and Kitchen, *cover photograph and plan of Blaydes House*. The University of Hull, Department of Adult Education. Messrs. Francis Johnson and Partners, *plan of Maisters House*. The City of Wakefield Art Gallery and Museums, *figs. 220, 221*. The National Monuments Record, *figs. 63, 64*. The Public Record Office, *fig. 47 and Title page Cartouche*. The following maps are based on the Ordnance Survey, *figs. 45-47, 49-52, 197*. The plans on pages *21, 22, 27* and *80* were especially drawn for us by Mike Grice and Roy Wilson of the Planning Department of Beverley Borough Council and to them we are particularly grateful.

Except for the illustrations above-mentioned the photographs and drawings were done by I. Hall for Messrs. Blenheim Fine Art Slides.

Frontispiece: Prince Street looking west.

INTRODUCTION

The Stuart precedent – 1650-1700

THE ARCHITECTURE AND CRAFTSMANSHIP OF HULL are not widely known, even in the area, partly because of the toll of two world wars and subsequent clearances,[1] in part because there has been no consistent attempt to survey the city's architectural heritage either for its own sake or, prior to demolition, as a record. Hence our book must consist largely of the photographic evidence needed as the vital basis for any assessment of Hull's still diminishing historic fabric and the subtle gradations of its particular historic character. The great mass of documentary evidence has always been more jealously guarded and hence will be more readily accessible to future historians. The three most important groups of documents are the archives of the Municipal Corporation of Hull, of Trinity House and of the Memorials of the East Riding Land Registry now incorporated into the Humberside County Record Office. To these should be added the relevant parish records, and the muniments of the great families whose patronage was a vital component in the life of Hull. There are too, such printed sources as newspapers, and the contemporary witness of the eighteenth and early nineteenth century writers of histories and guide books. We are conscious of the fact that we only touch upon subjects worthy of a monograph— one may instance Hull silver or Hull furniture— but in the absence of such we must point the way.

Kingston-upon-Hull, built at the junction of two rivers (*fig.* 268), occupies a site that is both a challenge and an opportunity— a challenge because the river Hull is still a barrier and an opportunity because the angle between the two rivers can be fortified (*fig.* 188) so as to defend a substantial trading community, which, on the one hand could look seaward toward northern Europe and on the other toward the river basins of the Trent, the Ouse, the Hull and their many tributaries. Hull, as it is usually called, was at the centre of a web of trading routes, 'importing' and 'exporting' a range of goods far in excess of its own immediate needs. As a comparative late-comer its inhabitants had to face the competition of centres already established, for example near at hand there were Beverley and York, and it was not until the eighteenth century that Hull craftsmen seized the initiative and developed new industries successfully, for example paint, furniture and textiles, that satisfied both a growing home market and began successfully to penetrate into those foreign markets where Hull merchants were already familiar figures. This duality in the trading pattern was to be reflected in both the architecture and the furniture of Hull, and it is these subjects, rather than a general history, that shall concern us.[2]

The influence of Ancient Rome, and for a time, Ancient Greece, forms the consistent background for the whole of English classical architecture, but as might be expected from a port with trading interest in the Low Countries, there was also the usual crop of Dutch gables and moulded brickwork. French influence is however, usually associated with aristocratic works in London rather than with northern England, yet in both eighteenth and nineteenth century Hull, anglicised forms occur (*figs.* 43, 44). There is too the important part played by craftsmen using the raw materials readily available to them. Wood carvers for example could work upon buildings, upon furniture and (*figs.* 110-113) upon ships[3], and because Hull was long a leading timber port, they had a splendid choice of woods, but stone masons were less well favoured because of the high costs of transporting good building stone from the quarries of the West Riding. Their opportunities changed dramatically after the onset of the Industrial Revolution — for carvers then had to face strong competition from mass produced and synthetic materials (*figs.* 182-187), while stone-masons could only welcome the quick, cheap transport of stone by canal and even more by railway. Likewise the comparative scarcity of wrought lead resulted in the virtual absence of the splendid early and mid Georgian lead rainwater heads to be found further west, and in the use of simple wooden divisions for fanlights instead of the lacy cast lead

[1] *See Note References on pp. 116-117.*

patterns found elsewhere (*cf.* the row of wood fanlights 17-29 Albion Street and of the lead one at 18 Land of Green Ginger).

The primary crafts were equally well placed, yet even here Hull practice differed from the usual run, for wood panelling remained in vogue until the 1770's, (*figs.* 120, 123-128) that is until patrons began to prefer printed wallpapers (Half title, *fig.* 162). Splendid doorcases too, were the joiner's rather than the mason's province (*figs.* 68, 71), and much of what seems painted stonework is usually of painted wood, e.g. the carved panels once on 8 Charlotte Street and those remaining on 22-28 George Street (Browns) (all built by Edward and Thomas Riddell). Even window cills are often only baulks of painted oak or pine. Bricklayers abounded, for there were ample deposits of usable brick clay including one from which a creamy white brick could be made, and this was a fashionable alternative to red stock brick from the 1780's onward, especially for country villas, such as that of the Pease family at Hesslewood. In the following decades when stucco was in vogue, a fine white brick served as an acceptable alternative for town terraces — such as Queen Street and along suburban roads such as Park Street, Spring Bank and Beverley Road (*figs.* 204, 211, 233), a choice matched by the use of stone for window cills and heads, string courses, plinths and doorcases (*fig.* 202). There was no substantial tradition of decorative wrought iron work and the abundance of timber slowed down the introduction of structural cast iron work for factories and warehouses, though cast iron was the inevitable choice for the balconies (*figs.* 239-242) and area railings (*figs.* 246-248) that became a familiar feature of the New Town that was to develop after 1780.

The concept of Old Town and New marks yet another difference between Hull and most other English cities and the term 'Old Town' is still in use to this day, much as it is in Edinburgh, but the New Town of Edinburgh was coherently planned — a process thoughtlessly rejected in Hull to its long-term detriment. This failure to think on a public rather than a private scale was to be echoed in the modest achievements in public buildings and in the architecture of new churches (though not one might add, in that of

FIG. 1   *Wilberforce House, entrance gates, c.1660.*

new chapels). Only the Trinity House of Hull, among public bodies, proved consistent patrons of the arts (*figs.* 141, 153).

The Old Town retained its physical isolation until the 1930's when the Queen's Dock was filled in. Before then the three 'town docks' marked the outline of the medieval moats (*fig.* 53), that prefaced the town's defensive brick walls, and towers, protecting Hull on the north, west and south. The fourth or eastern sector was defended only by the River Hull which, in the medieval period was far wider than at present, and which despite many objections, was subjected to such persistent encroachment that the 'harbour' was often reduced virtually to a standstill before the opening of the first dock. This weakness of the eastern flank prompted Henry VIII to build the citadel in 1541, a complex that was to survive in part until the 1860's, serving in the interim as a solid barrier not only to the development of the eastern bank of the river but also to the redevelopment of the Old Town itself because the latter had no through traffic. Once the problem of traffic flow was coupled to the spirit of 'improvement' the future of the Old Town as a recognisable entity was put in jeopardy. Many of the improvement schemes of the 1870's proved abortive, but the implementation of their twentieth century successors has reduced much of the Old Town to an unoccupied waste.

The street pattern within the medieval walls was essentially a network of new streets overlaying the few older tracks that led toward Hessle and Beverley. The parish church of Hull had been in the former village and the latter was an important town whose other link with the Humber estuary was via the River Hull. Naturally enough the new port had to follow the curves of the river bank (*figs.* 47, 48), which would need strengthening as trading increased. Wooden piles and sheet planking were the common reinforcement (some of medieval date have been recently excavated in Chapel Lane Staithe)[4] with brick walling as a more expensive alternative, the latter perhaps also serving as a foundation for half-timbered construction. As individual businesses grew, the more ambitious sunk piles into the river bed and on these extended their warehouses, a process to be

FIG. 2 *Wilberforce House, Tower porch, c.1660.*

repeated until the nineteenth century (see the weather-boarded warehouses built over the quays in *fig*. 48). This east side of High Street retained its high property value until 1778, thereafter to decline and thus to come under less pressure for wholesale redevelopment. The other main thoroughfare, the Market Place, was a long thin enclosure, a mere widening of a central street, with a Guildhall closing it at the southern end, and with the High Church, Holy Trinity, placed nearer the northern end of the west side. This was to become the Parish Church only in 1660. Further north still there were the substantial remains of the Manor House and of St. Mary's Lowgate (*fig*. 17). The former had been started by the de la Poles, but handsomely remodelled by Henry VIII (according to tradition, at the sacrifice of the western and central portions of St. Mary's truncations disguised by a new brick tower in 1697), its site became building ground in the earlier 1700's.

Elsewhere, by the mid-seventeenth century, the streets were lined by half-timbered houses, typically of one or two storeys, except for the houses of the wealthier, who could afford three or four. The medieval grid of streets in effect allowed for long thin gardens behind the houses, though as the population grew, more and more gardens were built over for houses and workshops (*figs*. 31, 33), a process that left frontagers with no option but to build upward. Some rebuilt from the ground, but perhaps as many built higher on top of existing walls or demolished only the front rooms (*fig*. 19), rebuilding on a more generous scale, a method of reconstruction that resulted in a fashionable front, but one that did not lose the owner too much business. The latter process was startlingly revealed by the recent demolitions in Market Place (*figs*. 19, 24), Queen Street and Mytongate (*figs*. 5, 25) which all contained medieval houses successively overlaid by panelling and plasterwork of seventeenth, eighteenth and nineteenth century date.

On the surface Hull exchanged its half-timber for brick — but the older constructional method survived in two places. Firstly many later medieval houses had indeed had timber frames, but with a brick infill (*fig*. 3) the vertical timbers were so shaped and spaced, and the bricks so made and laid that they formed a strong but thin and economical wall — a practice that survived until well into the Georgian period. The other context was in the design and construction of multi-storeyed warehouses (*figs*. 190, 191). The technique, with its inherent flexibility, could cope with heavy but variable loading, yet not impose massive weights upon foundations built on to Hull silt. The obvious risk was of fire, especially when oily goods were being stored or processed on the confined sites typical of High Street.

The latter had the merchant's house-cum-counting house next to the street with a through passage into the yard behind, as at Wilberforce House (*fig*. 28), next came one or more warehouses, then the board walk of the staithe with its hoists and big wooden framed cranes (*fig*. 48). Where the house went back a considerable distance, light wells or 'courtings', as they were called in older deeds, had to be incorporated as an essential part of the design. Good examples survive on the southern block of Wilberforce House, and their value is illustrated in an agreement of 1745 made by Christopher Pryme with Sir Henry Etherington. The former was rebuilding the frontage house of 52 High Street and agreed to leave his neighbour's courtings unobstructed by higher buildings.

Most staithes were privately owned and jealously guarded, but there were a few to which the public had access. Goods were brought ashore either direct from the ship, or by lighter, and taken away by horse-drawn sled or cart. Given the restricted access to the staithes, the customs officers found it difficult to collect the King's dues, so that in the 1770's the Government forced the issue and demanded the building of a legal quay.

Meanwhile Hull largely remained within its walls and as sites became congested the wealthier bought or rented 'garden spots' (*fig*. 53) within or without the town boundaries. We can see from Hollar's bird's eye view of Hull[5] that in the 1640's most houses had gables toward the street, but our knowledge of the house fronts of the 1660's onwards suggests that by then, designers preferred a horizontal eaves line broken perhaps by a tower porch (*figs*. 2, 13, 16). The modest houses of the

FIG. 3 (opposite, above left) *Mytongate, timber framed partition wall.*   FIG. 4 (opposite, above right) *Spring Street, section of house.*   FIG. 5 (opposite, bottom left) *Mytongate, Coach & Horses, detail of ceiling.*   FIG. 6 (opposite, bottom right) *9 Dagger Lane, rear elevation.*

HULL SILVER
FIG. 7 (opposite, above left)   *Tankard by Edward Mangie.*   FIG. 8 (opposite, above right)   *Tankard by Thomas Hebden, c.1684.*   FIG. 9 (opposite, centre left)   *Dish by Thomas Hebden.*   FIG. 10 (opposite, centre right)   *Detail of* FIG. 8. FIG. 11. (opposite, bottom left)   *Two spoons, one by Edward Mangie.*   FIG. 12 (opposite, bottom right)   *Porringer by Thomas Hebden.*   FIG. 13 (right)   *Silver Street, Ye Olde White Harte.*

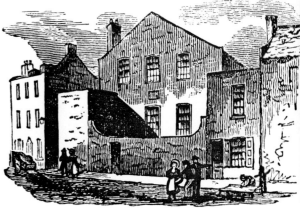

FIG. 14 (above left) *Façade by S. Serlio.* FIG. 15 (above right) *Dagger Lane Chapel, 1698, from Greenwood's View.* FIG. 16 (centre left) *Crowle's Hospital, c.1661, from Greenwood's View.* FIG. 17 (bottom left) *Lowgate. St. Mary's Church Tower, 1697, from Hadley's View.* FIG. 18 (bottom right) *Market Cross, 1680-82, Hilbert's View.*

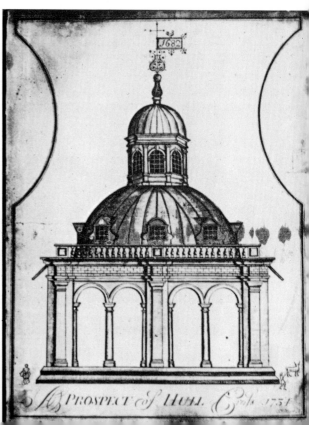

1660's that were recently demolished in Finkle Street had simple brick detailing and squarish window openings, with the long axis parallel to the eaves, but at Wilberforce House and Crowle House (25 and 41 High Street) the window openings were, in the Italian manner (*fig.* 14), symmetrically set with an emphatically vertical emphasis. Decorative motifs included cornices with one course of bricks, laid diagonally, cut brick jambs (both of these can still be seen at the rear of 52 High Street, an infill building of c.1660) bold overall rustication at Wilberforce House (*fig.* 2) and arch rings, brackets and pediments in finely moulded brick at Wilberforce House and Ye Olde White Harte off Silver Street (*fig.* 13) and the now demolished former Coach and Horses, Mytongate (*fig.* 26). This repertory was extended by Italianate wall panelling ingeniously created by recessed strips of brickwork to serve as a frame work as seen in Ye Olde White Harte. Traditionally both the latter and Wilberforce House date from the 1640's but on the evidence of comparable dated work the facades at least are post-Restoration. Since the bricklayers of Hull did not seem to

Fɪɢ. 19 (below) *Market Place, east side, prior to demolition in the 1960's.* Fɪɢ. 20 (right) *Market Place, King William III by Peter Scheemakers, 1734.*

indulge in carved brickwork, architectural features such as pilaster capitals and 'jewels', plaques and other small ornaments had to be carved in stone. The much illustrated Dagger Lane house also boasted a splendid Dutch gable[6]. The larger buildings with their pilastered fronts seemed to owe more to the woodcuts of books such as Sebastiano Serlio's *Archittetura et Prospettiva* (*book* 7, *p.* 10, *fig.* 14) published in 1619. (Serlio also showed how to turn an irregular old front into a smart new one.)

Only the Coach and Horses retained its contemporary staircase, which swept upward from ground floor to roof. Its compartment was a narrow rectangle, but the wide graduated steps gave an impression of spaciousness while easing the climber's task. The exceptionally tall newel posts and balusters used the Mannerist trick of inversion (*fig.* 23) a favourite motif found also in the Jacobean art of the previous generation. Upward movement was stressed by aligning the mouldings with the slope of the handrail. Only the deep handrail was of oak, the rest pine. Elsewhere fragments of carved decoration were found during demolition (in 1973) when the open moulded and beamed ceiling also came to light above the plain Georgian plasterwork (*fig.* 5).

Other examples of seventeenth century interior decoration of uncertain date are the re-used panelling at Maisters House (where it had survived the fire of 1743) and at Bayles House, 46 High Street. Later seventeenth century panelling was more self-consciously architectural in design (*fig.* 24), for it followed the basic proportions of the Orders. Hence the dado corresponds to the temple podium, the main panels to the column shaft and the room cornice follows, but often much more closely, the entablature over the columns. Where height permitted the room 'cornice' had the usual sequence of architrave, frieze and cornice. Staircases had turned and carved spirally twisted balusters, a typical Baroque motif, while doorcase and panel mouldings were boldly curved so as to stand proud of the wall surface, thus catching the light and creating a strong pattern of light and shade in rooms that were still rather low and under-lit by later standards, and it was against such a background that the smoothly gleaming surfaces of Hull silver-ware were intended to be seen (*figs.* 7-12).

Gold- and silver-smiths were certainly established in Hull by the fifteenth century but their heyday was really between 1620 and 1720. During this period Hull had its own town mark — not quite officially perhaps, but one that allows us to identify an interesting group of craftsmen. Unfortunately dating is difficult because there was no effective sequence of date letters for most of the period. The chief makers during the years 1680-1720 were Hebden and Mangie. Mangie evidently mended

FIG. 21 (left)   *6 Fish Street, detail of staircase by Hewitt, 1775.*   FIG. 22 (centre)   *Mytongate, detail of staircase, c.1730.*
FIG. 23 (right)   *Mytongate, Coach & Horses, detail of staircase, c.1660. (All demolished.)*

Corporation silver, being paid 8s. 6d. in 1680 for repairs. As at York and Newcastle, a few pieces follow Scandinavian or North German types, notably the peg tankards such as the one in the collection of Hedon Town Council. (The peg tankard was of ancient origin, and according to tradition was the invention of St. Dunstan, a tenth century Bishop of London, who in an attempt to improve men's manners, graduated the interior of communal drinking vessels by insertion of a row of pegs — hence the phrase to take a man down a peg or two.) The typical Hull piece is of satisfyingly simple shape, with engraved or repoussé ornament on the more important items. Well cut contemporary inscriptions and armorials also catch the light and so emphasise the adjacent polished surfaces.

FIG. 24 (above left)   *Market Place, detail of panelling, c.1690.*   FIG. 25 (above right)   *Mytongate, detail of panelling, c.1730-40.*   FIG. 26 (bottom left)   *Mytongate, Coach & Horses, courtyard, c.1660.*   FIG. 27 (bottom right)   *203 High Street, detail of re-used panelling, c.1730. (All demolished.)*

FIG. 28 (above) *23-25 High Street ('Georgian Houses' and Wilberforce House.* See also figs. 1 & 2. FIG. 29 (bottom) *Mytongate, north side.* FIG. 30 (opposite, above left) *Blanket Row, north side.* FIG. 31 (opposite, above right) *Plan of Scott's Square, 1757, built by Joseph Scott.* FIG. 32 (opposite, bottom left) *Humber Street, entrance to Scott's Square, 1757.* FIG. 33 (opposite, bottom right) *Scott's Square, surviving houses.*

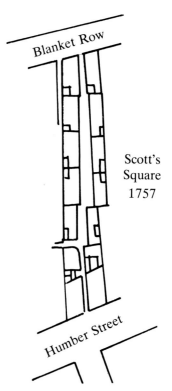

Scott's
Square
1757

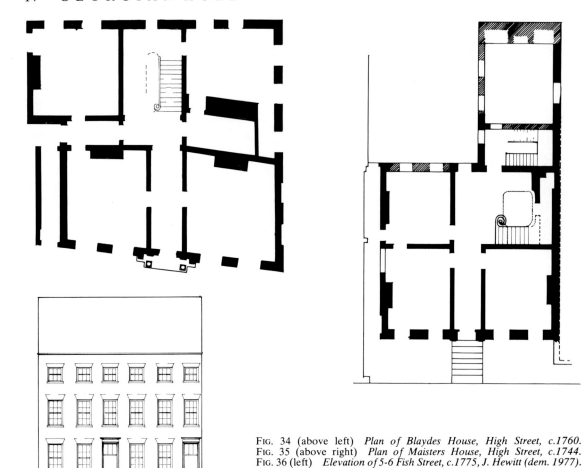

FIG. 34 (above left) *Plan of Blaydes House, High Street, c.1760.*
FIG. 35 (above right) *Plan of Maisters House, High Street, c.1744.*
FIG. 36 (left) *Elevation of 5-6 Fish Street, c.1775, J. Hewitt (dem. 1977).*

The most notable public building of the Baroque era was the Market Cross of 1682 (*fig.* 18) and the Bench Books reveal part of the story of its erection,[7] as well as much other detail of contemporary building activity in Hull. The Cross was erected at the substantial cost of £1,700 and was almost certainly the work of Richard Roebuck, a stone-mason. The municipal corporation's favoured architect of the period was William Catlyn who was paid £13 for supervision of the work. He also surveyed corporation properties, and planned, refurbished or rebuilt them where necessary. He remodelled the Guildhall in c.1682. (He is also known to have designed Brigg Grammar School.) For new buildings Catlyn submitted 'draughts', presumably a front elevation and floor plans, and for this he was paid a fee of a few guineas. He was paid £230 for building three new houses in Squirrel's Entry in 1682, but of these neither building nor record remains.[8-9]

It seems that the bench decided in 1679 that they would repair the old Market Cross, but by 1680 they were discussing building a 'cubilo', that is a dome, and making an agreement with Richard Roebuck, a 'free'-mason. A small committee was appointed to oversee the project, order materials, etc., among the latter 'marble stones' and clinkers for the floor, both to be imported from Holland. Roebuck was paid £100 and granted his freedom gratis, presumably in lieu of a fee for his design.[10] The Atkinson brothers, who had contracted for lead work, claimed to have made a loss and were given an extra 20 shillings for their pains. The Cross was however thought to be a traffic obstruction and was demolished in 1761. Hilbert's view of the Cross shows a substantial cupola and octagonal lantern on a square base of two pairs of arches framed by pilasters, and an open balustrade. Roebuck's composition had less dignity than Christopher Kempster's contemporary Town House at Abingdon (1680) though its dome and lantern were more exciting than the hipped roof crowning Henry Bell's Custom House at King's Lynn (1683).

Charitable works included the building of Crowle's Hospital in 1661 (*fig.* 16) with its handsome but distinctly provincial brick front in what Sir John Summerson has dubbed Artisan Mannerism, and the Charity Hall built in 1698, engraved in Hadley's *History of Hull.* The engraving shows a deep courtyard seven bays by five, opening toward Whitefriargate, with a hipped roof and pedimented dormers, a generous cornice and three tiers of nearly square casement windows, the whole typical of the urban architecture of the day rather than specifically of Hull. It differed from its contemporaries in its austerity — for most managed at least some decoration of their doorcases but in Charity Hall they were round arched, nothing more. (The site was sold in 1852 and the Branch Bank of England built in its stead.)[11] Littlewoods now occupies the site.

Not all was plain however, for there is a good series of finely carved cartouches such as that to Henry Maister (*fig.* 26) a group that evidently took the eye of Thomas Earle who quite unexpectedly for the 1820's reproduced the Baroque lines in monuments such as that to William Haddlesey at Hemingbrough near Selby. Among the few houses left of this period is 9 Dagger Lane (*fig.* 6). Nineteenth century stucco hides the brickwork, much as adjacent houses once concealed the pair of sharp gables of their rear elevation, but the front has the hipped roof characteristic of the day. This half medieval, half modern form of construction survived in part because gables were cheaper to build and roof, and because such economies went undetected from the street (*cf.* the biggest contemporary houses in Beverley). Brickwork now became much simpler, but to compensate, the best work had bricks chosen for uniformity of colour, shape and texture laid with fine joints in white putty. No contemporary doorway survives in Hull, but if Beverley examples are relevant, then doorcases were simply lengthened window openings, with flat rubbed brick arches, and door and window joinery came almost flush with the wall surface. Windows had leaded casements fixed to a central wooden mullion or to a cross-shaped mullion and transom. By the 1730's the fashionable preferred sliding sashes and insisted upon them throughout, but the more economically minded rewindowed only the front, retaining the older form elsewhere.

The pattern of development
1650-1850

HOLLAR'S VIEW OF SEVENTEENTH CENTURY HULL reveals that within the walls there were large areas of garden, but a century later the gardens of the Old Town were to be steadily built over with courtyard houses, euphemistically called 'squares', and Hull had begun to spread out into the township of Myton and the adjoining parishes of Sculcoates and Drypool (*fig.* 53), but only the development of Sculcoates now survives in recognisable form. Because the same craftsmen often undertook both infill and new development, the whole topic will be outlined here.

That the piece-meal Georgian rebuilding within the walls left some of the larger half-timbered houses still standing, can be seen from J. J. Sheahan's mid-Victorian description of High Street (1865).[12] The replacement of the oldest houses there can sometimes be traced through the indentures of individual properties, as in the case of No. 52 the Pryme mansion, offices and warehouses whose documentation reveals the site's building history from the mid seventeenth century to the present day, indicating how part of the rear garden of the frontage house was the subject of an infill in the 1660's (which remains today behind the subsequently twice rebuilt frontage property).[13] Alternatively, a

'Great Messuage' with its garden could be bought by a speculative builder such as Joseph Scott, bricklayer, who in 1757, acquired one whose site ran between Blanket Row and Back Ropery (*figs.* 31-33) (now Humber Street). New houses were built facing both these streets linked together by rows of cottage property (still partly surviving) in Scott's Square.[14] Similarly in 1756 Joseph Page (c.1717-1776) had bought the garden of Samuel Watson[15] (a sugar merchant) which lay between Holy Trinity and Dagger Lane. Page's plan[16] hinged upon the future of other properties in Priest's Row, west of Holy Trinity, but the municipal corporation proved willing supporters of a scheme for the improvement of the vicinity. The outcome c.1771 was King Street, linked to the charming curve of Prince Street (*figs.* 170, 171, 191, frontispiece) by a handsome archway. (The east side of King Street is long demolished but Prince Street fortunately remains.) The original plan probably envisaged houses on both sides of Prince Street, but the southern side was chiefly occupied by gardens, though Charles Mountain, the architect/plasterer, built at its eastern end, and it seems possible that the latter together with Thomas Hudson helped to provide resources for the development. Charles Mountain himself lived in the street,[17] as did another builder, George Jackson. The pediment and Venetian window on the King Street facade seem to be the first used on a Hull house front. Nearby in Fish Street, Joseph Hewitt,[18] a joiner, was building houses (*fig.* 36) in the former garden of 66 Mytongate where other joiners, Messrs. Hammond and Riddell were also to erect the Fish Street Chapel.[19]

The density of developments such as these can now best be judged by examination of the Ordnance Survey map published in 1855. There is evidence that the names of courts such as Pycock's Gallery or Stubb's Square[20] commemorate the speculations of their builders, but they were not the only ones indulging in speculations of this kind. For example the Broadley family bought and later redeveloped a large part of the remaining grounds of Suffolk Palace, an awkwardly shaped site just within the north walls. The position however became an advantageous one because it was close to the new dock and R. C. Broadley (d. 1812), decided to develop this property during the building boom of the late 1780's, employing George Pycock (1749-1799) to carry out the survey, and to lay out as building ground Manor Street, Broadley Street, Ann Street, Robert Street and Quay Street.[21] The plots were taken up by a variety of craftsmen, but only a few of the houses they erected now survive on the western side of Manor Street. The southernmost house, 18 Land of Green Ginger (*fig.* 201), was probably built by William Ringrose c.1790, for William Lee (merchant), and is much grander than the average[22]. Nearer the dock in Quay Street there were to be commercial premises such as those of Messrs. Casson and Stickney, makers of ships biscuits, and Joseph Outram for whom Pycock built extensive wine vaults. The development of the Pathway off Bowlalley Lane was instigated by a Mr. Cook (a gaoler), and it was then known as Cook's Square. Further east still, in Lowgate, George Pycock himself bought two frontage houses with large gardens for the substantial sum of £2,000[23] in 1784, and laid out the present Hanover Square on the site, building some though not all of the houses, while Samuel Hall was rebuilding the present 76, 77 Lowgate next door[24]. Meanwhile Edward Story (joiner, d. 1791) built Leadenhall Square on the part of the gardens that had formerly contained a leadworks.[25]

These developments may well have prompted yet another— that of Parliament Street (laid out by Mountain and Riddell) (*figs.* 197-199). An Act of Parliament was required because not all the existing owners proved willing sellers and the Act of 1795 included powers of compulsory purchase. The site included Mughouse Entry, whose inhabitants had long been the cause of distress to the more genteel residents of Whitefriargate (though some of the houses had only been built in the 1750's by Thomas Rosindale)[26]. The first proposal was for a tontine, to raise £21,000, involving among others Trinity House because it was claimed that the new street would enhance the Inn then building in Whitefriargate (*fig.* 154), but war damped the investor's enthusiasm and only a third of the money was raised. Sites were auctioned on 24th August, 1796, and fetched from just over £5.0.0 per sq. yd. in Whitefriargate to £2.5.0 for the less popular sites nearer the Dock. The Broadleys bought nine sites, the remainder being mostly taken up by six of the town's builders[27].

FIG. 37 (opposite)   *160 High Street, Maisters House by Joseph Page, 1744.*

The biggest development in the Old Town however was for the area between the southern end of the Market Place and the foreshore of the Humber (c.1804). Once again compulsory purchase powers were acquired by Act of Parliament in 1801. The scheme involved the demolition of premises as old as the town's Guildhall and the remnants of the Friary of St. Augustine, as well as new properties just completed for Trinity House (which the Corporation wished them to sell for less than the market price in order to persuade others to do the same in the name of public improvement). As in Parliament Street a uniformity of facade was thought desirable, but the Corporation laid down far more stringent conditions, including even the colour of the brick.[28] Only the centre pedimented block in Queen Street (24-27) survives (*figs*. 211, 217). By chance the project coincided with the excavation of the Humber Dock whose soil was dumped on the Growths as the Humber foreshore was called, and on this the Corporation laid out Wellington Street, Nelson Street and Pier Street (*figs*. 208, 268). However the recommencement of war with France slowed down the pace of building here as elsewhere in the town, and work was to drag on till the 1830's, though the land was obviously desirable for it fetched on average £1.10s. a sq. yd.

The first and much the most prominent of the new buildings here was the Theatre Royal, Humber Street (*fig*. 217), built to the designs of the younger Charles Mountain (1773-1839) in 1809. The pattern of housing here did not show the uniformity of elevation demanded in Queen Street. The building of the present Princes Dock in the 1820's provided yet another spur to the redevelopment of this side of the Old Town and designs still exist for terraces of proposed shops and houses that were to be built on the New Dock side.[29]

If the Old Harbour had concentrated wealth and interest in the eastern side of the Old Town, the creation of Queen's Dock (1774-78) (*fig*. 175) proved to be a vital turning point in the development of the 'New Town'. A map[30] of Hull and Sculcoates prepared for the government in 1715 at the time of the Jacobite crisis, clearly shows the few scattered dwellings that then existed outside the walls, and though there was some building along the newly created turnpike road to Beverley (Chariot Street) in the 1740's it was not until the 1760's that the Grimstons of Kilnwick thought fit to encourage the development of one of their three closes immediately outside the walls in Sculcoates. They leased the westernmost to Joseph Page (Field 16 G, *fig*. 45) who after difficulty over letting his new houses paid his first rent of £90 to John Grimston in 1767.[31] The first houses were in Waterworks Street and Chariot Street (the latter recalling Hustwicks, the coach builders) but the development was taken up after Page's death, by Timothy Fishwick, Edward Story, Robert Cross and others who built rows of humble houses all long demolished.[32]

Further east the new Dock Company saw an opportunity to augment their income by auctioning off their surplus land in 1781 and 1787 (*figs*. 45, 49-51, 175), part of closes 17, 18 and 19, 20, 21 and Trippett). They employed their Dock Surveyor, Mr. Holt, to lay out the new roads and Charles Mountain the elder to devise a suitable pattern for the facades.[33] Here the Dock Company followed the practice of contemporary land owners in London, though of course in the capital there were also the stringent restrictions embodied in successive London Building Acts. The spine of the new development was to follow an existing public highway from Beverley Gates to North Bridge and took the line of Savile Street, George Street and Charlotte Street (now also called George Street), and their extensions, North Street and Bridge Street, a line that included awkward angles (*fig*. 175). Land prices were not high[34] — especially in Charlotte Street where the grandest houses were to be (*figs*. 176, 177, 180), but the uniformity and elegance proposed for those in George Street and Savile Street was something never before attempted in the Old Town. There was however to be no coherent pattern of development to cover those fields and closes that had now become potential building ground, nor was there any attempt to reserve good sites for the churches and public buildings that would inevitably follow once the 'New Town' had got well under way, and there was only one owner, the Rev. Robert Jarratt, who was public spirited enough to lay out the present handsome Kingston Square (c.1801) in order to raise the tone of his own and neighbour's properties (*figs*. 200, 222-224).[35]

Fɪɢ. 38 (opposite)   *160 High Street, Maisters House, stairwell by Joseph Page and Robert Bakewell, 1744.*

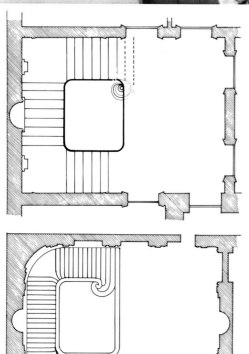

MID GEORGIAN CARVED CHIMNEY-PIECES
FIG. 39 (above left) *Maisters House, 1760's.* FIG. 40 (above right) *Formerly High Street (now The Old Rectory, Winestead).* FIG. 41 (centre right) *Formerly 18 Blanket Row (now The Old Rectory, Winestead).* FIG. 42 (bottom right) *Formerly Etherington House, High Street (now The Old Rectory, Winestead).* FIG. 43 (centre left) *Plan of Maisters House staircase, 1744.* FIG. 44 (bottom left) *Plan of staircase after Blondel, 1737-38*

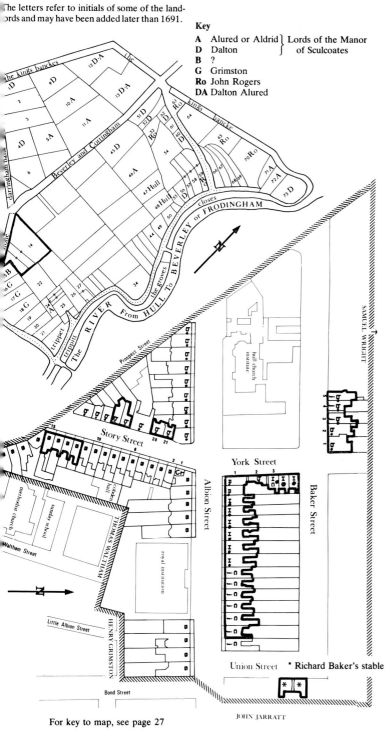

FIG. 45 *A Survey of Sculcoates of 1691* (redrawn 1849).

The letters refer to initials of some of the land-
lords and may have been added later than 1691.

Key

A	Alured or Aldrid ⎫ Lords of the Manor
D	Dalton ⎭ of Sculcoates
B	?
G	Grimston
Ro	John Rogers
DA	Dalton Alured

Sculcoates' Survey

		A.R.P.
1	Thomas Dalton, Esq.	8.2.30
2	Mr. Dickinson	
	Tythe free	9.3.0
	Stockdale Closes	
3	Town of Hull	9.3.10
4	Thomas Dalton, Esq.	12.1.0
5		
6	Thomas Dalton	9.0.0
7	Thomas Dalton	
8	Thomas Dalton	
9	Thomas Dalton	
	Great House Close	10.1.0
10	W. Apeland	17.0.3
11	Grt Apeland	40.0.0
12	Thomas Dalton, Esq.	
	Great Pasture	13.2.0
13	Thomas Dalton	
	Great Ings	33.1.0
14	Catlin	(29...17)
15	Mr. (Grimston) Myton	2.0.20
16	Mr. ——	3.1.0
17	Mr. ——	6.2.18
18	Mr. ——	
	Alford Close	10.0.0
19	Vaux Tyth free	6.1.10
20	Mr. Popple free	4.1.0
	God's Close	
21	Vaux Tyth free	6.2.5
22	Clement	10.1.2
	Little House	
23	Clement now Mr. Mason free	
24	Vaux Tyth free	
25	Vaux Tyth	3.0.0
26		6.2.1
27	Mr. Jno Burstall	
	now Ed Johnson	6.1.3
28	Mr. Jno Clemitt	
29	Mr. Jno Clemmitt	
30	Mr. Bewlay	
31	Town of Hull	
32		
33	Thomas Dalton &	
	Jno Purver now solely	
	Purver free	
34	Christopher	
35	Tho. Dalton, Esq.	
36	Aldrid Tyth free	
37	Thomas Dalton, Esq.	
38	Thomas Dalton	10.0.0
39	Town of Hull	
40	Thos. Dalton & Jno	
	Knowling	
41	Tho. Dalton & Jno Knowling	
42	Tho. Todd	
43	Tho. Todd	
44	Tho. Todd	2.3.0
45	Tho. Dalton, Esq.	20.1.0
46	Tho. Dalton	21.0.0
47	Town of Hull	9.2.10
48	Town of Hull	9.3.0
49	Manor House	2.0.0
50	Lady Wise	7.0.29
51	Thomas Dalton, Esq.	8.3.0
	Little Ings?	
52	Thomas Dalton, Esq.	3.0.0
53	Rogers Tyth free	4.0.0
54	Rogers Tyth free	
	Westfield 3 lands	19.2.0
55	Lady Wise	4.0.0
56	Thomas Dalton, Esq.	3.3.16
57	Thos Dalton, Esq.	
58		
59	Heirs of Rogers	
	Tyth free	
60	Thos. Dalton,	
61	Thos. Dalton	
62	Thos. Dalton	
	Little Pasture	
63	Heirs of Roger	
	Little Closes	
64	Lady Wise	
	Caves Closes	
65	Mr. Jno Roger	
	Tyth free	
	(Mr. Robert D	
66	Thos. Dalton,	
67		
68	Tyth free	
69	Tyth free	
70	Tyth free	
	North Field 3	
71	Tyth free	
72	Tyth free	
73	Thos. Dalton,	
	Green Fields 3	

For key to map, see page 27

FIG. 46 *The development of the Baker Estate on the southern close of Chaterhouse
Ings Magna, No. 14 on fig. 45. Story Street (east side) and Albion Street (south side,
east of Story Street) are of 1788-89. Albion Street (south side, west of Story Street) and
Story Street (west side) are of 1796-1803. Albion Street (north side, east of York
Street) is 1795-97 and York Street (east side) is also 1795-97 except No. 2 which is
of 1820. Baker Street is 1810-24. No. 19 Story Street was Mrs. Bennison's school.*

erring
the

Harker Bros.
Kingston Wharf
80 High St.

Morison &
Hawkesley
Brush Works

Mi

Brochner
4-46 High St.
(anish Buildings)

43- High St. -42

41 High St.
(Crowle House)

Bishop Lane
Staithe

Corn Exchange

Sykes

St.

James T. & N. Hill
Russia Merchants
11 High St.

Saltshouse Lane
Staithe
Site of Drypool Bridge
opened 1889

James T. & N. Hill

South End   Site cleared for   *Dog & Duck*   *Old Ferry*   *Brotherton*
       South Bridge 1862-65   *Boat Landing*   *Tavern*
                                                                        Rotten
                                                                          Sta

Etherington   *Scale Lane   47 High St.*
   Buildings   *Staithe*   *4*
                                                                       (L

Pease Warehouse   *Pease Warehouse*   *W. Beadle*
     1745   *1760*   *& C*
                          Bolton & Burman   *17 High*
           18-21 High St.

FIG. 48   *Frontages to the River Hull from Southend to North Bridge redrawn from photographs of c.1864.*

High Street—Owners of staiths and frontsteads from the Stone Chair to South End 1772-73.

Map ref.		*Map ref.*	
A	Mr. Maister, merchant	36	King's, coffee house
B	Ald. Blaydes, shipbuilding	37	Mr. Syke's, iron merchant
C	Mr. Walton, shipbuilding	38	Captain Coat's, oil merchant?
D	Kirkman's and Holgate's	39	Mr. Williamson's, iron merchant
1	Road to the bridge	40	Scale Lane staith
2	Mr. Blayde's yard, shipbuilding	41	Andrew's
3	Mr. Walton's yard, shipbuilding	42	Lambert's
4	Mrs. Fenley's	43	Alderman Etherington's, merchant
5	Mr. Bower's, mast and block maker	44	Mr. Prime's, merchant
6	Mr. Thompson's	45	Mr. Kirkman's
7	Mr. Blaydes	46	Mr. Taylor's, merchant
8	New Staith	47	Mr. Hickson's
9	Mr. Thompson's, merchant	48	The Charterhouse
10	Denton's (late Lawson's) Test's and Denton's frontstead	49	Mr. Bell's, merchant
11	Alderman Porter's, merchant Mingay's staith now Porter's	50	Mr. Lee's, sailmaker
12	Staith and Mingay's – now Porter's	51	Mr. Master's
13	Standidge & Stockdale, merchant & mariner	52	Church Lane staith
14	Mr. Rennard's, sugar refiner	53	Mr. Neave's
15	Mr. Pease's, oil merchant	54	Corporation's
16	Mr. Dixon's, timber merchant	55	Mr. Lee's, cork merchant
17	Alderman Parrot's & Collector's, merchant	56	Thomas Broadley, Esq., merchant
19	Mr. Hambleton (or Hamilton), tar merchant	57	Mr. Horner's, merchant
20	William Wilberforce, merchant	58	Mr. Burrel's
21	Mr. Kirby, brandy merchant	59	Mr. Milson's
22	Mr. Horner's, merchant	60	Mr. Watson's, merchant and sugar refiner
23	Mr. Howard, tar merchant	61	Mr. Shield's
24	Mr. Bealby, lead manufacturer	62	Mr. Christian Bell's
25	Alderman Thompson, timber? merchant	63	Mr. Barroby's, ship owner
26	Staith (Chapel Lane)	64	Mr. Ward's
27	Mr. Travis, tobacco manufacturer	65	Mr. Hickson's
28	Alderman Mowld, iron merchant	66	Mr. Pryme's
29	Custom House	67	Mr. Etherington's
30	Mr. Ray's, merchant	68	Mr. Etherington's
31	Isaac Broadley's, merchant	H	Rottenherring Staith
32	Mr. Pease	J	Charterhouse
33	The Hawk, public house	K	Crumpton's, ironmonger
34	Bishop Lane staith	L	Ellworth's
35	Captain Keld's and Alderman Cookson's	69	Horse staith
		N	Corporation House and South End

Note. This survey of 'staith and frontsteads' in High Street is compiled from the survey printed in Hadley op.cit., p. 688-89 and the survey by Joseph Page and John Broughton, drawn out by Thomas Chippendale, junior, which are both of 1773 and were found to match exactly. Trades are mainly from other sources.

PRO/MPD55

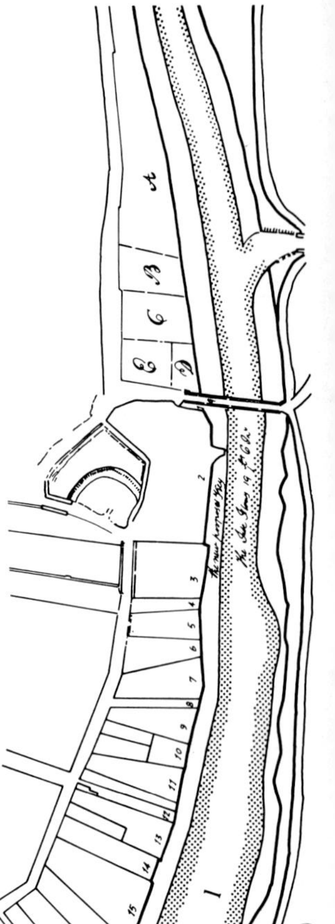
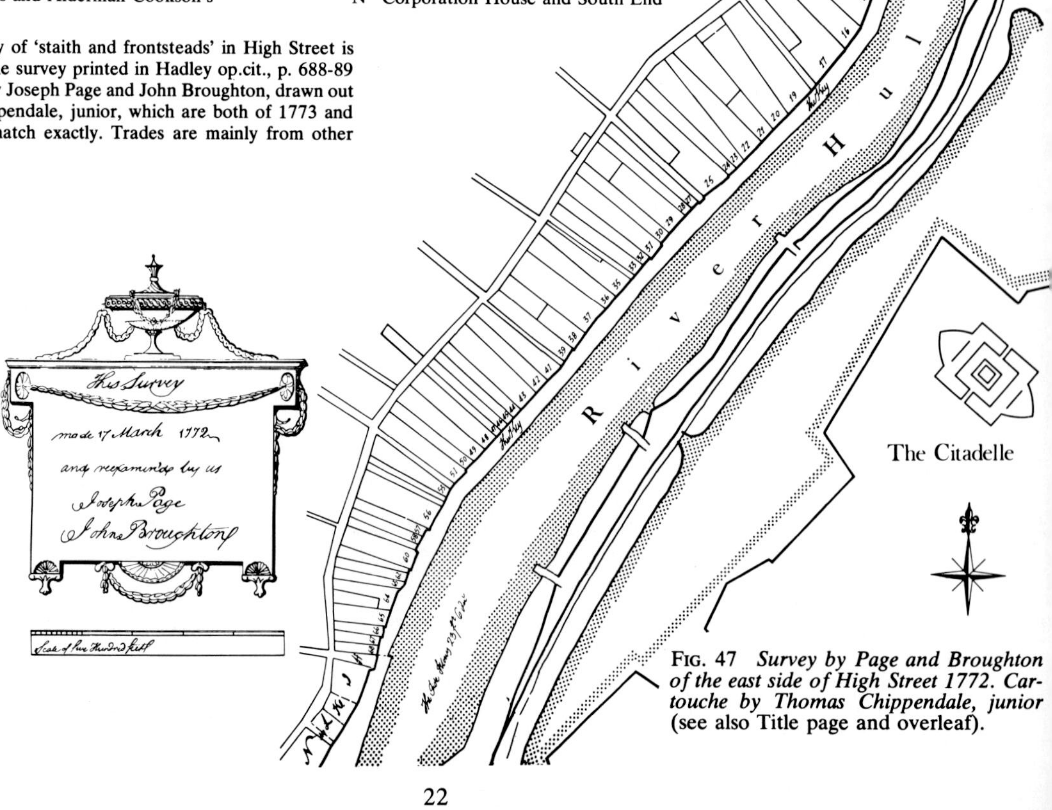

FIG. 47 *Survey by Page and Broughton of the east side of High Street 1772. Cartouche by Thomas Chippendale, junior* (see also Title page and overleaf).

:sq. 8.2.0
4.2.3
0.10 & 8.2.0
1.3.32
8.2.0
9.2.20
lton)
sq. 2.0.0
3.3.0
3.3.0
3.3.0
18.0.0
nds
4.1.25
6.0.0
sq.
ands

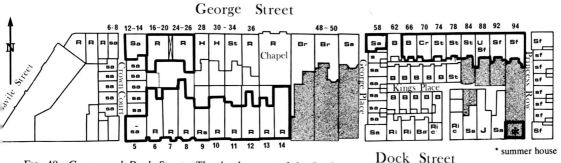

George Street

FIG. 49 *George and Dock Streets. The development of the Dock Company Estate, 1788-98.*

Dock Street

* summer house

Charlotte Street Mews

FIG. 50 *Charlotte Street (now part of George Street). Original numbering.*

FIG. 51. *Savile Street.*

Nelson (Garden) Place

Nile Street

FIG. 52 *The development of Nile Street (south side). For elevation,* see fig. 207. All houses are now demolished. The street plan—and possibly the elevations—were drawn up by Joseph Hargrave, arch. and carver.

KEY for figs. 46 (p. 21), 49, 50, 51, 52

Developers

B	Broadley, C. E.
Br	Bromby, J.
DC	Dock Company
G•	Green, H.
G	Green, J.
G	Green, P.
H	Howard, J. & R.
L	Lambert, C.
M	Moxon, R.
O	Osborne, W.
P	Pease, J. R.
ES	Saner, E.
Rs	Savage, R.
Sf	Staniforth, J.
W	Walker, J.
W	White, T.

Builders

Ap	Alcock & Preston, builders
Ba	Bambrough, R., builder
B•	Bennison, A., mason
C	Clarkson, B. & J., joiners
Cr	Cross, R., joiner
FU	Fox, J. & Usher, T.
H•	Hopewell, D., mason
J	Jackson, G., bricklayer
K	Kidd, Daniel, bricklayer
M	Mountain, C., Sen.
Rn	Nevis, R. surveyor
Pa	Parkin, G., bricklayer
Ri	Richardson, R., bricklayer
R	Riddell, E. & T.
R•	Robinson, T., builder
Sa	Savage, G., builder
S	Story, Ed., joiner
St	Stubbs, S., plasterer
T	Truefitt, J.
U	Upton, W. & Edmund, H.
V	Vickerman, T., plumber

garden

Georgian buildings still standing

The main sources used in compiling the maps showing street development are the Memorials in the Registry of deeds and the Sculcoates Rate Books (City R.O.) 1786-96, 1797-1805, 1806-12, 1813-19.

27

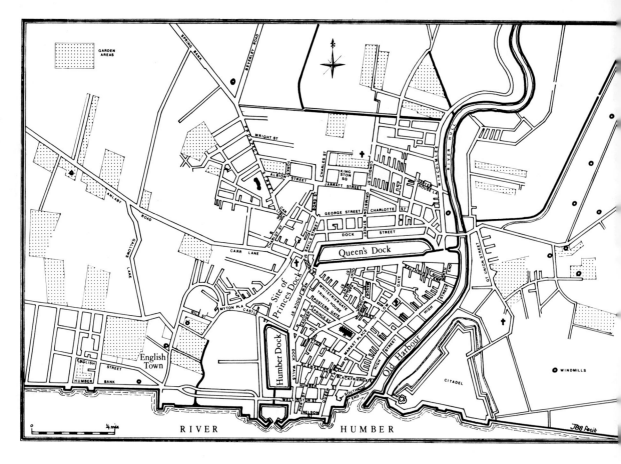

FIG. 53. *Mountain's Plan of Hull 1817 (redrawn).*

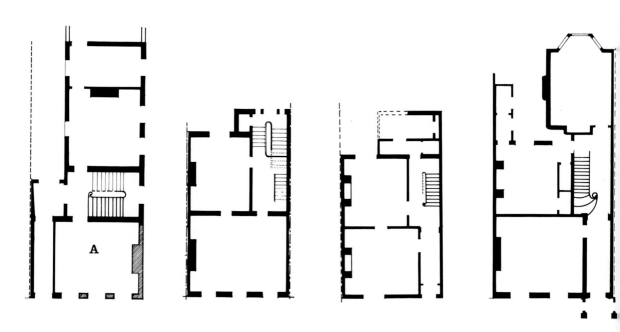

FIG. 54 (left)   *Plan of 203 High Street, c.1757.*   FIG. 55 (centre left)   *Plan of 33 Posterngate (first floor), 1764-65.*   FIG. 56 (centre right)   *Plan of 8 Pier Street, c.1824.*   FIG. 57 (right)   *Plan of 55 Park Street, c.1845.*

In the case of George Street and the developments behind it, the level of the land was raised by excavation material from the New Dock. Further north-east the scheme meant the loss of French's Garden for the sites of Mason Street and Sykes Street, and that of Thomas Knowlton (one of the leading gardeners of his generation, working for the Earl of Burlington and among others advising William Constable on the improvement of his gardens at Burton Constable) who had sold his close to the Dock Company (*fig*. 175).

In the absence of contemporary architects' drawings one can only follow the progress of the New Town through the Memorials in the Land Registry. In those cases where a merchant had bought a plot of building land for example, Richard Howard, a tar merchant in Savile Street (*fig*. 51), it is often difficult to find out who built on his behalf, and if he had enough capital, there need be no urgency for him to sell, unlike the situation facing the speculative builder, who could not afford to allow too much of his capital to be tied up in bricks and mortar. In practice most of the new houses were probably built up by a consortium of different tradesmen, each pooling their skills and the materials of their trade. It appears for example that Edward and Thomas Riddell (joiners) and Charles Mountain (plasterer and architect, 1743-1805) worked together on much of the Dock Company estate. Sometimes a mortgage would be necessary. On other occasions a banker such as Joseph Robinson Pease would put up the necessary finance to builders whom he could trust — for example, Fox and Usher in Charlotte Street (*figs*. 50, 180) — and together they would then sell the property.[36] Pease himself built the grandest of these new town mansions No. 12 (1783) to the designs of Mountain (who surely also designed 14 and 15 Charlotte Street) (*fig*. 77) and he noted that he had spent about £10,000 upon building and furnishing it and its flanking neighbours (13 and 11), whose facades were integrated with that of Pease (*fig*. 176),[37] but this striking terrace of houses on the north side of Charlotte Street was not completed until 1800. Extraordinary as it may seem, these, the grandest of Hull's houses, overlooked timber

FIG. 58.   *High Street, north end.* (Left) *No. 202;* (centre) *former Dock Office;* (foreground) *Blaydes House.*

yards and the Queen's Dock though the commercial boom that followed the ending of the war with Napoleon, encouraged speculative builders to build here too. The development in Dock Street (c.1792) is largely attributable to the building family of Riddell and their houses were less self-consciously grand though in their day elegant enough within and without (see for example the still surviving interiors of 7 and 8 Dock Street). As in Charlotte Street the Riddell houses had their share of pediments (*fig. 203*). Between the parallel blocks of George Street and Dock Street (sold off in the third auction of Dock Company land of 1787) there was to be courtyard housing and these too had simple if well designed elevations and internal detailing, and like their counterparts built by Riddell to the west of Savile Street (Riddell's Entry later Admiral Place), they seem to have been inhabited largely by mariners (*fig. 284*).

Further north Richard Baker (tobacco manufacturer) bought the southern part of the old close, Charterhouse Ings Magna (*figs. 46, 204*) from the Jarratts in 1787,[38] developing Story Street and the south side of Albion Street with Edward Story and Appleton Bennison (1750-1830) the mason, architect. The remainder of Albion Street was the work of several builders who none the less gave it a surface uniformity (*fig. 196*).

However if anything characterises the whole of this new town development it is the consistent refusal to build to the strict uniformity implied by a terrace. Just why this should be so is not clear, though the situation was readily accepted by contemporary commentators, one of whom — Tickell,[39] describes Story Street as 'a handsome range of houses' while of Albion Street (south side) he says 'a single row of houses; they are built upon a regular plan . . . so that this street when finished will be one of the most elegant and ornamental in town'. The west side of Story Street was given a unity of design by a pediment on the largest house (Mrs. Bennison's School), the same motif being used for the

FIG. 59 (bottom) *High Street, Blaydes House, staircase, c.1760.* FIG. 60 (opposite, above) *Blaydes House, 'Tabernacle Room'.* FIG. 61 (Opposite, bottom left) *Blaydes House, entrance hall.* FIG. 62 (opposite, bottom right) *Blaydes House, entrance front, c.1760.*

STAIRCASE IN Nº 51

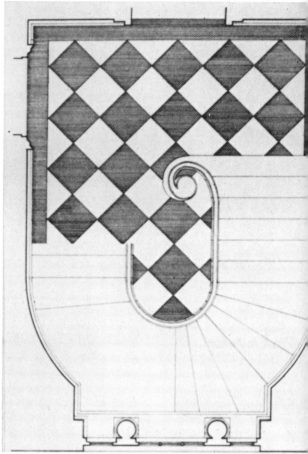

FIGS. 63 & 64 *High Street, Etherington House, Section and plan of staircase hall.*

'eyecatcher' 23-27 Worship Street, built by John Fox (1806) to terminate the still important view along Albion Street—Jarratt Street (*fig. 223*).[40]

It was perhaps fortunate that Hull's builders seemed content with minor changes in architectural style, so that a change from one builder to another during the infilling of the many gaps in the various streets did not result in too great a change in the pattern of the elevations, though one may detect nuances when a stonemason such as Appleton Bennison replaced a joiner such as Edward Story. Typical Bennison houses are the infilled garden now 2 York Street (c.1820)[41] whose elevation was manipulated so as to permit two entrances to the back yards (*fig. 202*), and the block 1-5 Baker Street (*fig. 204*).

On the fringe of this part of the New Town building proved desultory and for a long time groups such as 1-11 Wright Street (c.1803-24, *fig.* 205) must have seemed strangely isolated, as must many groups of houses in what the late Georgians called English Town, in Myton, near the Humber, where the occupiers must frequently have had the advantage of uninterrupted views across the river toward Lincolnshire. Equally good views of shipping were claimed for the row of houses probably designed by Joseph Hargrave and mainly built by Robert Nevis in Nile Street (c.1804, *fig.* 207). These houses had the further advantage of facing across a charming garden shared with Marine Row (*fig.* 52), a selling point mentioned in contemporary newspapers.[42]

If the Napoleonic Wars created problems for the speculative builder they also provide a convenient water-shed in the history of urban development, for as in other rapidly growing northern towns such as Manchester, there was to be a significant post-war shift in favour of front gardens and consequently those streets for which these had not been planned in front of the houses could no longer claim to be in the forefront of fashion. As early as the 1780's the Riddells provided front gardens in Riddell's Entry (*fig.* 51), and subsequently in front of the houses in Portland Place, a novel idea that soon became standard practice in houses of respectability. In the 1820's Caroline Place was advertised as having this amenity[43] (the eastern end still survives) and the newly laid out streets around Spring Bank and Beverley Road were for the most part laid out with small front gardens, the back garden frequently also being integrated in the manner of the day as a logical extension of the house (a process advocated by writers such as Humphry Repton and J. C. Loudon) (*figs.* 57, 270).

The development of Myton from 1783 onwards in the area between Prospect Street and Nile Street was of a more urban character — though the development of two major landowners, the Broadley family and Trinity House involved the building over the nurseries of the Portas family. The new streets joined up with

FIGS. 65 & 66   *46 High Street, Bayle's House staircase, c.1751.*

DORIC PORCHES

FIG. 67 (above left) *Dock Office Row, Oriental Buildings (former Dock Office), c.1820.* FIG. 68 (above right) *High Street, Blaydes House, c.1760.* FIG. 69 (bottom left) *Albion Street, Dr. Alderson's house, c.1845-46, see fig. 88.* FIG. 70 (bottom right) *Charterhouse, c.1779-80.*

Fig. 71 (above left)   *Formerly 21 High Street, Perrott House, now at Leven, c.1745, Corinthian doorcase.*   Fig. 72 (above centre)   *Haworth Hall, c.1760. Roman Ionic doorcase.*   Fig. 73 (above right)   *York Street/Albion Street, c.1820. Greek Ionic doorcase.*   Fig. 74 (bottom left)   *23-24 High Street, 'Georgian Houses', c.1751. Roman Ionic double doorcase.*   Fig. 75 (bottom right)   *81 Beverley Road, c.1832. Greek Doric porch. David Thorp, architect.*

Savile Street and Whitefriargate at the east, and Carr Lane and Anlaby Road at the west. Trinity House eventually developed their properties south of Carr Lane with houses and almshouses (*fig.* 156) while from 1801 the Broadleys started to lay out a grid of streets with Paragon Street[44] — a continuation of Waterworks Street — as the spine. Much of the property was of humble character and in consequence almost nothing now survives.

For the first thirty or forty years the New Town was regarded as an almost wholly residential development but the post war boom encouraged many to convert houses to shops and the proximity of the docks encouraged others to build workshops for the manufacture of furniture, etc. — movements that resulted in commercial as well as domestic infill. One such block survives — that on the eastern side of Savile Street (1827-30) and this westward siting of shops has continued gently ever since.

The Palladians 1740-1770

BY CHANCE THERE IS LITTLE TO SEE OF THE HOUSES built or reconstructed between 1700 and the 1740's, but thereafter we can find not only buildings, but gain some knowledge of the craftsmen involved and of their sources of inspiration. One might go further and claim that the mid-Georgian period brought out the best in Hull's craftsmen for they worked in a style that gave them scope, whereas the introduction of the brilliant Adam style from the 1770's provided them with something deceptively easy to imitate. Hence one can derive great enjoyment out of the interiors of the mid-century, but thereafter one becomes too much aware that designers were provincial followers of London fashions.

FIGS. 76 & 77 (opposite)   *25 High Street, Wilberforce House, details of staircase, c.1760.*   FIG. 78 (bottom left)   *Holy Trinity Church, detail of Rococo altar table, c.1753.*   FIG. 79 (bottom right)   *25 High Street, Wilberforce House, centre piece of drawing room ceiling, c.1760.*

Figs. 80 (above left), 81 (above centre), 82 (bottom left) *Holy Trinity Church, Rococo altar table and reredos.* Fig. 83 (above right) *Trinity House Chapel, altar table by Sir William Chambers, 1772.* Fig. 84 (bottom right) *St. Mary's Church, Sculcoates, font formerly a wine cistern from Hotham House, Beverley, c.1717 (cover later).*

The chief town mansions were still to be found in High Street and some advertised their opulence by having front doorsteps cut from massive blocks of black marble (*fig.* 68). Sadly only one set is now in situ at No. 6 (Blaydes House) but there was recently another at the Travis house, No. 196, just opposite. Marble floors, some of great squares of black and white (e.g. Blaydes House, *fig.* 61 and Etherington House 49/51 High Street, *fig.* 64), others of white with inset black dots at each corner were frequent (a surviving example but of stone and marble can be seen at No. 46). The former give a strong abstract quality, a hint of a Dutch interior, the others recall the plan of a Roman hypocaust, with the dots symbolising the square supporting columns and the joint between the white squares, the groin lines of the Roman concrete vaulting. Serlio illustrates the plan in book 3, p. 96 of his *Archittetura*. The standard house front was a severe sheet of brickwork, pierced by rectangular window openings — enlivened only by a handsome doorcase and thin bands of stone on the parapet and as a stringcourse and a deeper band for a plinth (*fig.* 37). Some houses also had stone keystones. Because the entrance doorway was often used for commercial purposes, imposing flights of steps were usually avoided. The inconvenience of business traffic was sometimes reduced by opening a discreet side entrance such as those at Blaydes and Maisters houses and at Alderman Jarratt's house in Lowgate. A later alternative at 76 and 77 Lowgate (c.1784) was to have an arched carriageway linking the street and the warehouse in the rear courtyard.

The comparative austerity of Hull façades reminds one of Dublin rather than of the showier fronts to be seen in York or Bristol or Liverpool, and as in Dublin, the visitor is subtly prepared for a surprise. In Hull it is the staircases. In 1756 Isaac Ware[45] advised his readers that a good house should have two staircases, 'one for show and the use of the company, the other for domesticks — when the principal door of the house is as it should be, in the centre, the staircase should present itself immediately beyond the hall (*fig.* 61). There is often an air of space and room in throwing back a staircase, and this may be done to such advantage in a moderate house, as to make it seem much larger than it is by a great part of it being seen first.' In a succeeding chapter (p. 487-8) Ware notes that 'there is no part of a house where the eye is more naturally directed upwards than the staircase: this is a reason why some compartition and ornament of the ceiling is in that part peculiarly proper'. . . . 'In a house any thing decorated, we shall advise our architect to recommend the giving of some embellishment to this ceiling — and if there be nothing else of the kind in the house it will still look well!' Though Ware was recording standard London practice he readily admitted that alternatives could also achieve a good effect. In Hull, the stairs at Blaydes House and at 33 Posterngate (1764) typify Ware's ideal (*figs.* 59, 61, 164) but those at Etherington House (c.1740) (*fig.* 63) and Maisters House (1744-45) (*fig.* 38) were even more spectacular.

By this time three Hull staircase plans had become standardised — for very restricted areas there were flights that simply passed and repassed (*figs.* 21, 23), where a square well was possible there could be three short flights per floor with a hollow square centre (*figs.* 22, 38), and where a generous rectangle was available two wide parallel flights were linked by a semi-circle scooped out of the half-landing (*figs.* 59, 65, 66, 164). In the first and second examples, joiners could either use ramps and newel posts at each turn — much the commonest pattern over England as a whole, or as a more local variant the hand rail could be worked into upward sweeping curves at each change of direction, and, where space allowed, terminate in a whorl at the bottom step (*fig.* 66). The curving hand rail is commonplace in Hull and to a lesser degree in the East Riding. Outside this area ramped handrails were generally preferred — the two types of construction overlapping at York. Plotting and cutting the sinuous curves of handrails taxed the joiners ability, but in a town of shipwrights the necessary skills were available.

There was too, a small group of staircases based upon the semi-circle and the oval — at Etherington House, the Pease mansion in Charlotte Street (1783), the second Dock Office (c.1820) and the Pilot Office (1819-20) all but the first of late Georgian date (*figs.* 63, 255, 257).

Etherington House staircase was fitted into an older shell and its unknown architect swept the eye upward, first by curving the steps into an apse with a fine Ionic Venetian window (of the kind sometimes favoured by William Kent) which accorded with Ware's description as being 'a kind

calculated for show and very pompous in their nature; and when executed with judgement, of extreme elegance'[46] (p. 467). All was crowned with a shallow dome on richly decorated pendentives. Such a treatment would have excited attention even by contemporary London standards, though domed staircases were to become a favourite treatment by the 1770's and 80's. The staircase has a neo-classical quality that suggests an acquaintance with the Burlingtonians, but the details of the carved balustrade, especially the concave sided knop on alternate balusters, repeat a motif also found at Beningbrough Hall (dated 1716) and at the Treasurer's House, York. The remaining rooms were refitted with new panelling, one with pedimented doorcases. Some of these fittings were rescued when the house was demolished after the Second World War and reinstated at the Old Rectory at Winestead (*fig. 3.7*).

Maister's House, was wrecked by fire in 1743, a calamity in which Mrs. Maister was

FIG. 85 (opposite, above) *Haworth Hall, south front.* FIG. 86 (opposite, centre left) *Haworth Hall, entrance lodge, c.1830.* FIG. 87 (opposite, bottom) *Haworth Hall, entrance front, c.1760.* FIG. 88 (opposite, centre right) *Albion Street, Dr. Alderson's house, c.1845-46,* see fig. 69. FIGS. 89 (left), 90 (bottom) *Haworth Hall, two views of principal staircase, c.1760.*

HAWORTH HALL, stucco decoration, c.1760-70.
FIG. 91 (above), *Dining Room*. FIG. 92 (centre) *Staircase Hall*. FIG. 93 (bottom) *Drawing Room (the right hand panel is based on a design by Sir William Chambers)*.

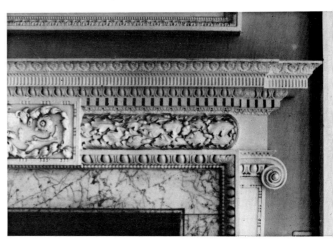

FIG. 94 (above left) *Haworth Hall, marble chimney-piece in Dining Room, c.1760,* see fig. 98c. FIG. 95 (above right) *Haworth Hall, carved wood bedroom chimney-piece.* FIG. 96 (centre) *Haworth Hall, carved wood bedroom chimney-piece after Sir William Chambers,* see figs. 98b and 99. FIG. 97 (bottom) *Haworth Hall, richly carved Drawing Room doorcase.*

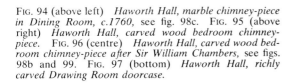

FIGS. 98a, b & c (above right) *Sir William Chambers 'Civil Architecture',* detail of plate opposite, p. 125. FIG. 99 (centre left) *Haworth Hall, east wall composition of bedroom over Drawing Room.* FIG. 100 (bottom left) *Haworth Hall, marble chimney-piece in Drawing Room,* see fig. 98a. FIG. 101 (right) *Haworth Hall, detail of fig. 100.* FIG. 102 (opposite, above left) *Haworth Hall, detail of palm tree windows in Drawing Room.* FIG. 103 (opposite, above right) *Sketch for Chinese room decoration at Burton Constable, c.1840.* FIG. 104 (opposite, bottom left) *Palm tree corner stand by Thomas Brooks at Burton Constable, 1842.* FIG. 105 (opposite, bottom right) *Sketch by Thomas Atkinson for a palm tree bay window. Burton Constable collection.*

FIG. 106 (above left) *Burton Constable, dragon carved by Thomas Brooks, 1840.* FIG. 107 (above centre) *Trinity House, 'Chinese' gas lamp, c.1830.* FIG. 108 (above right) *Burton Constable, Chinese porcelain stand by Thomas Ward, c.1840.* FIG. 109 (bottom left) *Burton Constable, chinese dragon chair by Thomas Ward and T. W. Wallis.* FIGS. 110 (opposite, above left), 111 (opposite, above right), 112 (opposite, bottom left), 113 (opposite, bottom right) *Burton Constable, carved wood decoration by Jeremiah Hargrave, 1767-69, after designs by Lightoler.*

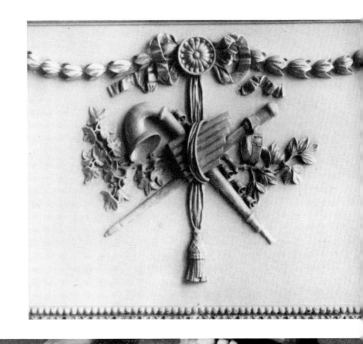

FIG. 114 (above)   *High Street, Blaydes House, detail of carved doorhead in dining room, c.1760.*   FIG. 115 (bottom)   *Burton Constable, detail of carved doorhead in Drawing Room by J. & J. Hargrave after designs by J. Wyatt, c.1777-78.*

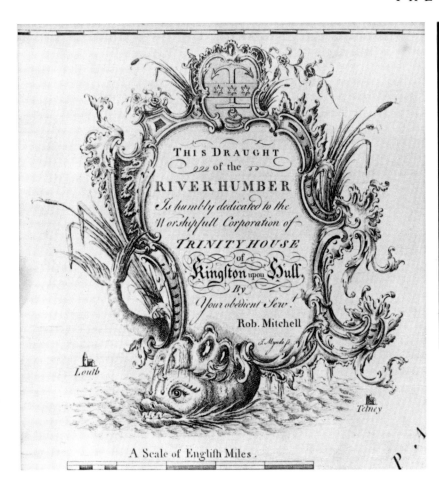

FIG. 116 (above left)   *Map cartouche with dolphins.*   FIG. 117 (bottom left)   *Burton Constable, bedroom chimney-piece by Hargrave after Lightoler.*   FIG. 118 (above right)   *Burton Constable, detail of fig. 117.*   FIG. 119 (bottom right)   *Lightoler's original sketch* for fig. 117.

Fɪɢ. 120   *203 High Street, sketch of panelled room at* A *fig. 54. West and South walls* see figs. 123-128.

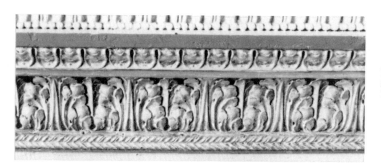

Fɪɢ. 121   *Burton Constable, carved dado rail in Drawing Room by J. & J. Hargrave. The architect's drawing is below.*

Fɪɢ. 122   *Burton Constable, drawing by J. Wyatt, 1775, showing doorcases, girandoles, etc. carved by J. & J. Hargrave,* see figs. 115, 121.

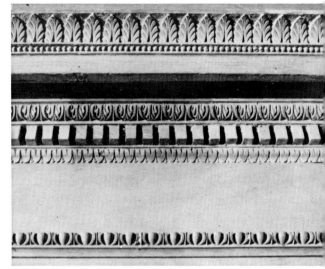

No. 203 HIGH STREET, carved details.
FIGS. 123 (above left)   124 (centre left)   *Dado rails.*   FIG. 125 (above right)   *Room cornice.*   FIG. 126 (centre)   *Skirting board (note overpainting to right).*   FIG. 127 (bottom left)   *Details of doorhead.*   FIG. 128 (bottom right)   *Details of south wall. Inscribed behind carving 'South Side front Tabernacle Pannill',* see fig. 126 and fig. 60 for earlier Tabernacle.

among those who lost their lives. Henry Maister rebuilt his house to the designs of Joseph Page. The latter had been apprenticed to Thomas Scott (bricklayer) in 1733 and took up his freedom in 1740. The facade was set back from the general line of the street and the front door given an imposing flight of steps (*fig. 37*). The door case was modelled on a plate in James Gibbs' *Book of Architecture*, published in 1728, and this Palladian doorcase in the manner of Inigo Jones, suggests a dignified interior, but the *tour de force* is yet concealed to view, for it opens off the right hand side of the hall. A rich and intricate wrought iron balustrade first catches the eye (*fig. 38*), then Cheere's statue of Ceres, the goddess of the harvest and then finally, looking straight up, a square balcony, a highly decorated coved ceiling and a domed octagonal lantern that pours light upon the whole composition. As so often,

TRADE CARDS.
FIG. 129 (above left)   *John Fletcher, engraved J. Hilbert of Hull, c.1750.*   FIG. 130 (bottom left)   *Thomas Meggitt and Son, engraved Goodwill & Lawson of Hull, c. 1834.*   FIG. 131 (above right)   *Hull and Leith Steam Packet Co., c.1845.*   FIG. 132 (centre right)   *Detail of William Taylor's (Beverley) card, engraved Goodwill & Lawson of Hull, c.1830.*   FIG. 133 (bottom right)   *Edmund Foster, engraved Terry, c.1770.*

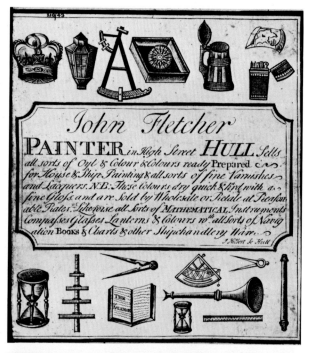

the doorcases here are of a pattern derived from William Kent's *Inigo Jones*[47] — a work to which many East Riding gentlemen had subscribed, including Lord Burlington who had himself ordered 12 sets, and we know from a letter of 1744 that his Lordship's advice had been sought regarding the decoration of the house and he recommended simplifying a cornice.[48] The architectural details are Palladian, but the ironwork was wholly to the design and workmanship of Robert Bakewell (1685-1752) of Derby. The finished balustrade, which reproduces Bakewell's favourite pattern, would be shipped from Derby to Hull via the Trent. The plan of the compartment itself is not Palladian for it owes more to French models such as those published by J. F. Blondel in his *Maisons de Plaisance* of 1737-38 (*figs*. 43, 44).[49] Page however confined his quadrant corners to the balustrade and they form a symmetrical central well when viewed from the second floor gallery. The sequence of dome, gallery, etc. might have been influenced by plate 7 of Isaac Ware's *Designs of Inigo Jones* which shows a section of the stair case at Ashburnham House, Westminster, a work then attributed to Jones. Again, if a London parallel is sought, one can only turn to Kent's masterpiece at 44 Berkeley Square built in 1742-44. Page's standard price-list for decorative plasterwork survives.

Rates of plaister by Jo: Page

Two Coates on Laths 2½ p yard on Walls 2d p Yard Do on Walls p yd Floated Sealings of fine Plaister 6d p Yard Do on Walls 5 d p Yard stucko from 6d p yd to 8d— Do Plaine Mouldings 4 d p foot or one penny p yd 4in in girt.— Cornich Mouldings Carved 2d p foot— Inrichd Architraves for Tabernacules frames 1 s 8d p foot — Ionick Modilions 3d apiece Do Corinthions 6 d — Panils for Sofits with Roses 4d a piece— Ionick Capitalls 7s 6 p— For 5 Bard Fretts 5d— Do for 6 Bard 6d for 7 Bard 7d — For Single Goulicohes 6 d p foot Do for double Goloches with with Roses & Huskes 9 d p foot — for Vitoulious Scroules 10d p foot Festones with Shelles or flowers 2s & 5d p foot — Foulidges for panils in Bastorelievo from 1s 2d to1s&6d p foot — Frizes adorned with Oakes & Acorns 4 p foot — 6 Inch Roses 3s Do 9 Inch 5s.— Do 12 Inch 10s— 18 Inch 16s— For 2 foot &half Roses £.1.1.s.

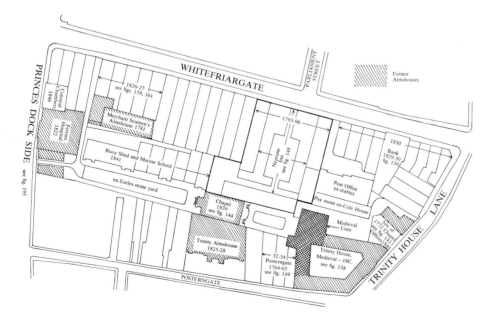

FIG. 134   *Plan of Trinity House, Whitefriargate Estate after William Foale 1859.*

FIG. 135 (above)   *Trinity House, detail of entrance front 1753-59, pediment by Hargraves, stonework by Rushworth.*   FIG. 136 (bottom)   *Whitefriargate, detail of former Smith's Bank, now Messrs. Woolworths, Charles Mountain Jnr. architect, Thomas Earle, sculptor, 1829-30,* see also fig. 150.

FIG. 137 (above)   *Former Ferries Hospital, Princes Dockside, pediment by Earle, 1822.*   FIG. 138 (bottom) *Trinity House, entrance front 1753-59, attributed to Jeremiah Hargrave, architect.*

TRINITY HOUSE, four views of the Court Room, 1773-75, Joseph Page, architect.
FIG. 139 (above left) *Ceiling.* FIG. 140 (above right) *Exterior from the east.* FIG. 141 (bottom left) *Interior looking south.* FIG. 142 (bottom right) *Interior, east wall.*

FIG. 143 (above left)   *Trinity House Chapel of 1772 from Hadley's View, Sir William Chambers, architect.*   FIG. 144 (above right)   *Trinity House Chapel 1839-43, east front, H. F. Lockwood, architect.*   FIG. 145 (bottom)   *Trinity House, Court Room, detail of entrance doorcase, J. Hargrave, carver, J. Page, architect.*

THE PRINCE OF ORANGE
BY CASPARIUS NETSCHER

The adjoining rooms are mostly panelled, with cornices and other mouldings clearly reflecting a hierachy of use from the counting house to the drawing and dining rooms. The latter has the finest double decker chimneypiece in Hull, its Kentian-Palladian frame[50] overlaid with brilliant carving of vines, nuts and other motifs appropriate to a dining room (*fig. 29*). It probably dates from c.1760 when Nathaniel Maister tried to persuade his friend John Grimston to buy an overmantel picture. Grimston replied that for a specially painted picture Maister could expect to pay much more than for one ready painted. The plain plaster walls were prepared for papering, then coming into vogue. (An even later amendment of c.1790-1800 was the insertion of a 'composition' chimneypiece in the ground floor room to the left of the hall. The figures on the jambs symbolise Love and Modesty after designs by George Richardson— a curious choice for one engaged in business life. Such figures were usually priced at 9d. each.)

After years of uncertainty the future of Maister's House is now safeguarded by the National Trust.

A little further north on the other side of the street, William Wilberforce's father faced the task of remodelling an older house. The old staircase was removed from the north wing, and a new one built to the south, opening off the central passage. A fluently Rococo ceiling panel catches the eye just inside the staircase door, its curving lines suggesting those of contemporary jeweller's snuff boxes. The marble floor and bold sweep of the carved and turned balusters and the Venetian window are characteristic of High Street, but the ceiling here is of exceptional richness (*figs. 76, 77*). The Wilberforce eagle is at the centre and symbols of the four seasons are on plaques in the corners, the remainder swirls with Rococo flower garlands and scrolls typically English in their underlying symmetry. The present drawing room has panelled walls with the wide shallowly moulded frames then popular in Hull. The chimney breast here has tall Ionic pilasters supporting a heavy entablature with its plump pulvinated frieze. The chimney piece itself is of c.1790-1800 and was brought in from a long vanished High Street house. The room to the east has reset panelling from the Perrott-Moxon House, 21 High Street, a house refronted and remodelled c.1745 and demolished just over two centuries later.[51] Nos. 23 and 24 narrowly escaped the same fate. They were built for James Hamilton, a tar merchant, shortly after 1756[52] and share a massive double Ionic doorcase beneath a broad triangular pediment— an unusual solution to the problem, though prior to the virtual destruction of this narrow street the heaviness of the pediment was less noticeable when viewed in perspective (*figs. 28, 74*). The identical staircases are simpler than that at No. 25, but are none the less like those that George Schonswar designed and executed in Posterngate c.1764-5 (*fig. 164*). Regrettably nothing seems known about the interior of the Pease house, No.18 (alas, demolished after the war). This is a pity

FIGS. 146 (left), 147 (right)   *Trinity House Court Room, two views of chimney-piece,* **J. Page,** *architect.*

because Joseph Pease was one of the wealthiest of the Hull merchants, the town's first banker and one who took the lead in industrial enterprise. Fortunately his splendid warehouses dated 1745 and 1760 just survive (*figs*. 48, 190, 191). Their scale can be judged by *fig*. 190 which shows the interior of the 1745 section.

The continuity of High Street has been severed by Alfred Gelder Street, leaving the northern end an isolated fragment. The panelled room of No. 194 fell a victim to the demolition of 1976, though an overmantel was rescued for re-use in Blaydes House and the once handsome but long neglected interior of the Travis House, No. 196, has totally gone. No. 203 was also demolished in 1976 (*fig*. 172), leaving only the boarded up shell of Nos. 201-202 out of a once dignified row.[53] Nos. 201-203 were built c.1757 for the Lawson family, though the Haworths were soon to occupy them (in the later Victorian period the site became Johnson's paint factory, the frontage houses becoming offices, a change which hardly affected the interiors). No. 203 was built on the site of an 'anchorsmith's workshop' whose gabled south wall was probably that revealed during demolition, incorporated in the lower part of its successor. Virtually every room was panelled though demolition disclosed fragments of a deep green wallpaper and border, overprinted with black and white, which had survived flanking the unpainted outline of a pedimented Palladian chimneypiece, which had been replaced by one of c.1775 in the Adam manner. At this latter date it was also decided to repanel the ground floor room at the corner of High Street and North Dock Walls, a room notable for its finely carved early neo-classical detail (*figs*. 120, 123-128). This 'transitional' style was repeated in another ground floor room whose carved chimney piece frieze repeated yet another of Kent's in Ware's *Inigo Jones*, but with a wholly Adamesque centre panel where Kent had left his tablet wholly plain. No. 6, Blaydes House, just across the street is no longer threatened with demolition and has been admirably restored by the Georgian Society for East Yorkshire (*figs*. 58-62). Though the building is now an architect's office, not a merchant's residence, the loan of appropriate furniture by Hull Corporation and others has brought back more of the feeling of a house than is usual. Blaydes chose a wide Doric porch set upon shallow, black marble steps, an elegant adaptation of the rather squat Tuscan design published by Batty Langley in 1739 (*fig*. 68). A fully detailed entablature with carved capitals and, for those who look up, a strip of rich fret, forecast yet more carving within. The plan (*fig*. 34) is simple, a central hall and staircase each flanked by pairs of rooms with a lobby between those on the left and the servants' staircase next to the kitchen, in the corresponding space on the right. The irregular placing of the chimney stacks on the latter side suggests that that quarter of the house may be an older survival, as does the unexpected picturesqueness of the gabled roofs outside, where, between the tall chimney-stacks, the remains of a belvedere look-out survives, from which the shipowner could spy the arrival of his ships in the Humber.

The front door like many others in Hull, has no fanlight, so that the entrance and stairs are both lit by the ornate Corinthian Venetian window on the half-landing. The stair balusters too, are opulently heavy with a gadrooned vase as pedestal for a baluster (much closer than usual to stone prototypes) but the scrolled foot and semicircular sweep of the handrail on the half landing must have given Blaydes' contemporaries a reassuring feeling of his firm's solid merit. As at Maister's House there is a hierarchy of room treatment. Here the counting house walls have a cladding of vertical boarding with joints overlaid by strips of simple moulding. The room to the east— the Tabernacle room (*fig*. 60), has a simplified 'Jonesian', chimney-piece overmantel and a recess with a segmental open pediment. The full Ionic entablature is confined to the chimney-breast. In the dining room the chief feature is the splendid Corinthian doorcase on which every moulding is carved (*fig*. 114). The half pilasters are an infrequent motif, yet one found in the work of both Sir Robert Taylor and Sir William Chambers, and this suggests a probable date of the 1760's, i.e. during a transitional period. As further evidence of this note the use of thick fleshy scrolls (*fig*. 59) and thin wiry ones on the stair-case ceiling. The latter also has tiny coved edgings whose shadows suggest that the ceiling floats above rather than bears down upon the beam and cornices. The principal chimney-piece in the house is of white and coloured marbles and as Ware suggests, these are left polished but not carved, to show off their beauty.

Not all High Street houses fronted the street, No. 46 (Bayles House) for example was described in 1751 as a 'house and accompting house, little yard or yards lying before the same house and the entry

and fore door and passage leading from the High Street up to the same messuage'.[54] In short No. 46 had two lettable houses next to the street and a profitable warehouse fronting the staithe eastwards. The façade is of fine red brickwork though with some Victorian alterations. Its chief feature is now the charming staircase, its elements carefully scaled down to enhance its real size (*figs*. 65, 66). The lower part of the staircase walls are left plain, below the band of Vitruvian scroll, but above this are three 'eared' panels, that opposite the Venetian window given a little extra enrichment. The arched part of the window is ingeniously inserted into the coved ceiling — the later subdivided into enriched panels in the manner recommended by Isaac Ware (p. 490).[55] The staircase itself has the treads and risers of the first flight projecting from the supporting wall, an East Yorkshire motif, but the upper flight is fully cantilevered, with triple panels beneath each step (*fig*. 66).

The surviving or recently surviving mid-Georgian interiors of Mytongate had simple

FIG. 148 (above) *Whitefriargate, Neptune Inn, G. Pycock, architect 1794 from Greenwood's View.* FIG. 149 (centre) *Posterngate, former Savings Bank and Nos. 33 & 34, latter Schonswar and Towers 1764-65.* FIG. 150 (bottom left) *Whitefriargate, former Smith's Bank block, C. Mountain Jnr., architect, see fig. 136.* FIG. 151 (bottom right) *Trinity House, wrought iron staircase, c. 1753-54, John Waugh, ironsmith.*

FIG. 152 (above left)   *Whitefriargate, former Neptune Inn banqueting room ceiling, G. Pycock, architect.*   FIG. 153 (above right)   *Trinity House Chapel ceiling, H. F. Lockwood, architect, 1839-42.*   FIGS. 154 (bottom left), 155 (bottom right), *Whitefriargate, former Neptune Inn, now Messrs. Boots,* see fig. 148.

panelling (*fig. 25*), chimney-pieces and staircases, though occasionally the latter had carved, iron twist balusters alternating with plainer ones. By the 1750's or 60's panelling was frequently confined to the dado, with the plastering above colour washed or wall-papered. (The cheapest paper, a plain blue is still sometimes found stuck to a wall.) The advent of the printed wall-paper marks an obvious change in interior decoration. Hitherto interior design had been in the hands of craftsmen but now more and more decorative finishes could be bought ready made, among them not only printed papers but papier maché, 'composition', Coadestone and textiles, whose selection and installation were not necessarily carried out by a building tradesman — but the decline in importance of the latter was perhaps slower in Hull than elsewhere, for the joiner and the woodcarver retained their vigour until well into the Adam period.

The Georgian churches and chapels of Hull have mostly been demolished and are now best studied in the engravings of Greenwood's *Picture of Hull* published in 1835 but there are also good accounts by Edward Ingram of the rebuilding of St. Mary's Sculcoates (*figs.* 84, 259) and the many alterations at St. Mary's Lowgate.[56]

The earliest of the chapels was that built in Dagger Lane in 1698 (*fig.* 15) and despite its many changes of occupant its plain brick shell, at least, survived intact until 1978 when the front was demolished. The majority of later chapels followed the standard formula of a central pedimented block flanked by slightly lower wings with ranges of round arched windows on both front and sides. Several of the plainer chapels such as that in Scott Street (1824) (*fig.* 265) were given Victorian embellishments in stucco.

The most regrettable losses are certainly the two chapels designed by H. F. Lockwood in Albion Street and Great Thornton Street, but Lockwood's still surviving chapel at Trinity House (*figs.* 144, 153) gives us a glimpse of his capabilities, for he was building at a time when classical churches were the subject of bitter criticism.

The Roman Catholic church of St. Charles, Jarratt Street was begun by John Earle (1778-1863), remodelled soon afterward by J. J. Scoles (1798-1863) and remodelled more dramatically yet again under the superintendence of Smith, Brodrick and Lowther, who added the porch shown in *fig.* 266. The calm exterior gives no hint of the Baroque drama within.

Meanwhile the older churches underwent the usual repair and beautification. Holy Trinity for example acquired a painted altarpiece by James Parmentier (1658-1730) and an exquisitely carved mahogany altar table and pine reredos whose main components fortunately still survive (*figs.* 78, 80-82). The grey marble slab was a gift of the Sykes family in 1753.

Craftsmanship

JUST WHAT PROMPTED THE WAVES OF BUILDING activity is not known, though it surely reflects both the growing trade of the port, the town and its hinterland as well as the rising prosperity of the countryside. Merchant and landowner alike seemed set upon change, remodelling older houses or building new ones. These opportunities were doubly important for the Hull craftsman, for while he might expect to gain work in Hull, he was up against fierce competition from contemporaries in Beverley and York for work in great country houses such as Burton Constable or Sledmere. Moreover, by the 1760's he was pitting his skills against London men who offered the finest

FIG. 156 (opposite, above left)   *Carr Lane, Master Mariners Almshouse, details of drawing by C. Mountain, Jnr.*   FIG. 157 (opposite, above right)   *Whitefriargate, unexecuted design by G. Jackson for Smith's Bank block.*   FIG. 158 (opposite, centre left)   *Sketch attributed to Thomas Earle for pediment in fig. 136.*   FIG. 159 (opposite, centre right)   *Whitefriargate, alternative design for 1826 block attributed to C. Mountain, Jnr., see fig. 161.*   FIG. 160 (opposite, bottom left)   *Formerly Posterngate, Oceanus by Thomas Earle, 1834, see fig. 144.*   FIG. 161 (opposite, bottom right)   *Whitefriargate 1826 block attributed to C. Mountain, Jnr., architect.*

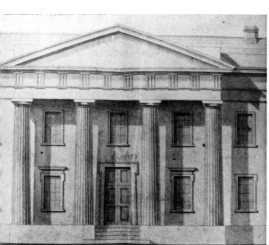

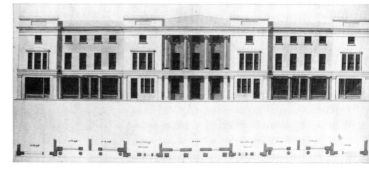

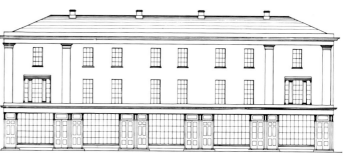

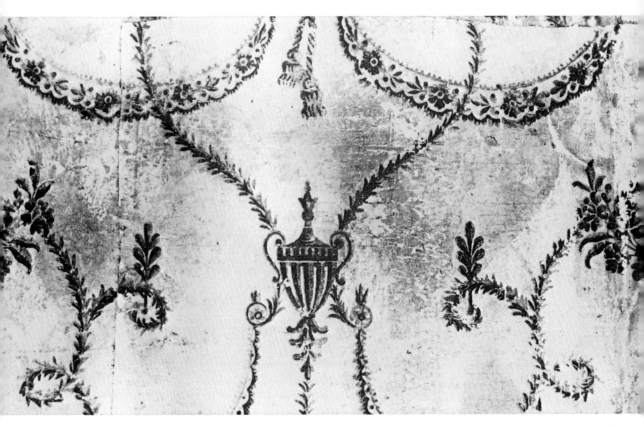

FIG. 162 (above) *33 Posterngate, wallpaper of c.1789.* FIG. 163 (bottom left) *33 Posterngate, detail of chinese Chippendale attic staircase.* FIG. 164 (bottom right) *33 Posterngate, principal staircase, Schonswar and Towers, builder/architects, 1764-65.*

Principal Craftsmen

Andrew Archibald, stone cutter.
John Buck, mason.
George Earle, paviour.
Jos. French, brickmaker.
Gelson & Fowler, carpenters.
J. Hargrave, architect & carver.
Walter Jenkinson, painter.
Josiah Milner, turner.
Charles Mountain, stucco.
John Norman, iron work.
John Shackles, upholsterer.
Towers & Jervis, builders.
William Wasney, ironmonger.
David Wharam, plumber.

FIG. 165 (above) *The Charterhouse, engraving after Joseph Hargrave, architect, c.1779-80.* FIG. 166 (centre left) *Charterhouse Chapel, detail of pulpit, J. Hargrave, carver, c.1779-80.* FIG. 167 (centre right) *Charterhouse Chapel, interior looking east, c.1779-80.* FIG. 168 (bottom) *203 High Street, detail of 'composition' chimney-piece, c.1770.*

FIG. 170 *Prince Street looking towards King Street arch, c.1771, Joseph Page, architect.*

craftsmanship in the shortest time, a competitive advantage difficult to match. The more ambitious Hull men responded easily to the challenge of technical skill, but they counter balanced their slower output by under cutting in price. This was the age of the 'proper workman' rather than the architect, as that term is now understood, and building projects were generally the combined effort of the tradesmen involved, each using his personal vocabulary of decorative motifs, each in discussion with his patron, selecting and adapting ideas culled from the many architectural treatises and pattern books of the day. The average craftsman could buy the latter for a few shillings a piece though not many could readily afford the more luxurious folios of engravings priced at several pounds, nor, unless they worked for the great landowner such as William Constable of Burton Constable (1721-91), could they get easy access to drawings submitted by well known London architects (*figs*. 115, 122). Once they had entered the charmed circle of such connoisseurs, treatises and drawings could be studied and discussed, and as their working acquaintance of great houses grew, so too did they gain invaluable first hand knowledge of current London taste, information that they could use to their advantage.

From the 1740's to the 1770's the prevailing style was Palladian, at first closely following the precepts of Inigo Jones, Colen Campbell, Lord Burlington and William Kent and others of Burlington's circle, but as elsewhere, by the 1750's plasterers and carvers introduced, first their interpretation of the Rococo style and then in the next decade, what they thought to be neoclassical motifs, with, as always, a confused overlapping when elements of the new had not really ousted their forerunners. Even the leading craftsmen had to diversify. Bricklayers were also trained as plasterers, some carvers (e.g. Jeremiah Hargrave 1726-86) had to tackle work in stone (*fig*. 135) or wood (*fig*. 145) and carve furniture (*figs*. 111-113, 117) or architectural joinery such as doorcases, chimney pieces, etc. as opportunity permitted. Those with a bent for draughtsmanship and a talent for site organisation could offer their services as designers and building contractors or supervisors, e.g. George Pycock — and these were the first steps toward the status of architect. The less ambitious stuck more closely to their trade, but in Hull, they often had to be prepared to take on other jobs altogether to eke out a living in hard times. Some advertised that they sold building materials (e.g. William Settle, joiner (fl. 1780-1821)),[57] others became publicans, grocers, etc. In good times a skilled craftsman could live well. For example Jeremiah Hargrave lived for a time in one of the better streets, Whitefriargate, and could afford to take time off to go to the races, and to indulge himself in the luxury of a bill made out on gilt edged paper![58]

As demand for skilled men grew faster than the supply of trained apprentices, Hull Municipal Council could not take effective action against 'foreigners' who set up their business in town. In contrast York and Beverley men feared outside competition and sought to force foreigners such as John Fisher or James Henderson to purchase their freedoms, or to go. In the mid and late Georgian periods Hull was a magnet that attracted craftsmen from both Lincolnshire and the East Riding (Joseph Page the architect/plasterer came from Lincolnshire and Thomas Walker (fl. 1760-94), cabinet maker, from Beverley) and conversely one can see how its specialist craftsmen such as veneer sawyers found employment as far afield as Thoresby in Nottinghamshire (which was being rebuilt for the Duke of Kingston 1760-70's).

It is tempting to draw quick comparisons between Georgian Hull and Georgian York and to point out the splendid achievements still to be seen in the latter city, but though York overtly courted the aristocracy, as can be seen by the Assembly Rooms, the Mansion House and numerous other town houses, the standard of rich craftsmanship, especially in skills such as wood carving and furniture making, was no higher than in Hull.

Both crafts were to be linked, as can still be seen in the state rooms of Burton Constable where the documented work of four generations of Hull craftsmen remains in situ. Carvers' and cabinet makers' names are recorded in various documents before 1750, but there now seems little likelihood of achieving

FIG. 171 *King Street looking towards Prince Street, c.1771, Joseph Page, architect.* See also frontispiece.

FIG. 172 (above left)   *200-203 High Street (The Lawson-Haworth houses), c.1756-57. Now partially demolished.*   FIG. 173 (above right)   *41-46 High Street, centre portion 1828.*   FIG. 174 (bottom)   *50 Salthouse Lane, former Branch Bank of England, c.1780.*

positive attributions, but from the 1750's we can trace the rise of Hull and the corresponding decline of Beverley and York as centres supplying the great houses. The alternative sources were Wakefield (from which Edward Elwick sent substantial quantities of furniture to East Yorkshire) and of course London. Lancaster was too far away for the Gillows to send furniture economically to the area. In effect this left London men as chief competitors. In 1764 the latter, unwisely, rejected William Constable's request that sketches be sent to him for the items he wished to have made.[59] Thenceforth he turned most often to Hull where he could find men to 'hearken to his wishes', but Constable was less sure of their ability as fine plasterers before Charles Mountain proved his competence in the 1780's and here the York men retained the lead, as is indicated by the Wilberforce House drawing room ceiling which has certain motifs (*fig.* 79) that recur in the handsome saloon ceiling at Bishophill House, York, recently removed to Peasholme House. A similar situation arose when the finest workmanship was sought for carving marble.

Constable employed Jeremiah Hargrave and Joseph his son, for most of their working lives and then briefly tried their apprentices Clark and Cowham. The Hargraves maintained a meticulous standard equal to that of London men, but unlike the latter, they ignored the fact that the finest detail as seen on the bench is of little consequence if it can scarcely be seen once the carving is in place. In contrast Chippendale's carvers realised that brilliant effects could be achieved more economically by adroit use of undercutting and bold clear outlines. By chance the Hargraves and the Chippendales were to become direct competitors at Burton Constable in the 1770's. In 1767-69 Jeremiah Hargrave had carved all the ornament (*figs.* 110-113) in the new Dining Room (except the dining tables and chairs) for a charge of £92. 2s. 4d. He worked to the sketches of Thomas and Timothy Lightoler, the carver/architects. Constable, who was a discerning and generous patron, persuaded his craftsmen to reject the rococo in favour of an Anglo-French neo-classical style, that was avant garde in its day, though later he turned toward the more conventionally English neo-classicism of James Wyatt or Thomas Atkinson (*fig.* 122).

One consequence of his patronage was the encouragement of the Hull furniture making industry at just the time when the enterprising could take advantage of the new dock and its adjacent timber yards. In 1766 for example, Constable was the successful purchaser of mahogany at a public auction, an exotic timber, that a little earlier had had to be brought especially from London, but once confidence grew in the potential opportunities offered by a furniture industry, a few timber merchants such as Dixon and Moxon set up to cater for a growing specialist demand. Soon they were supplying

FIG. 175 *Map of Dock Company Estate 1778 by Charles Tate (redrawn).*

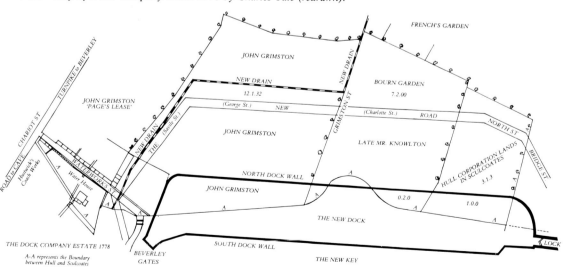

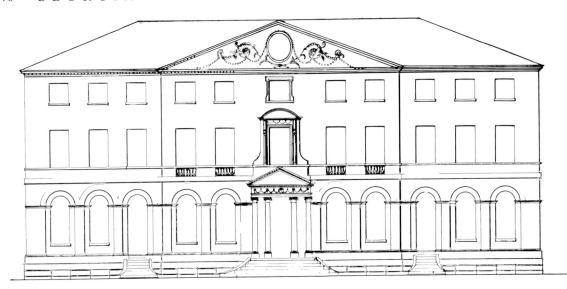

Fig. 176 (above) *11-13 Charlotte Street, built for J. R. Pease by Charles Mountain, architect.* Fig. 177 (below) *Charlotte Street, c.1910. The nearer houses by or attributed to Charles Mountain, 1783.*

mahogany to the great houses then being built in the north and midlands. (One less scrupulous adventurer offered mahogany at bargain prices, an offer that reached the ears of the Duke of Portland, then building at Welbeck. He sent his agent to secure the needed mahogany only to discover that the importer had had mahogany packing cases so made that they could be taken apart without damage, the timber then being offered at cut price.)[60]

Henceforth the York and Beverley furniture makers were put at a disadvantage for they had to add substantial transport costs to their overheads. Men such as Thomas Walker, trained by Charles Rawlins at Beverley, migrated to Hull, where he set up in business off Scale Lane and from thence he supplied Trinity House, the Corporation and Burton Constable. Works for such clients were almost

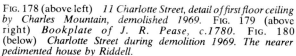

FIG. 178 (above left)   *11 Charlotte Street, detail of first floor ceiling by Charles Mountain, demolished 1969.* FIG. 179 (above right) *Bookplate of J. R. Pease, c.1780.* FIG. 180 (below) *Charlotte Street during demolition 1969. The nearer pedimented house by Riddell.*

certainly viewed by their makers as show-pieces, to display to potential patrons (who would be informed as to their destination), as well as to their trade rivals, who would either have to adapt themselves to the newer styles or perhaps suffer a decline in business. Before the end of the century advertisements[61] were put into Hull papers offering steady jobs to those who would try their luck in London, and Hull makers trade labels proclaimed not merely their training in London but 'for exportation'. Conversely eight Hull furniture makers subscribed to Thomas Sheraton's well known Drawing Book of 1791-94, including Thomas Walker. Hull firms were typically small family concerns rarely lasting three generations. Their output was slow, and because they had little capital they could not afford to make much furniture for stock, though as trading patterns changed during the later eighteenth and early nineteenth centuries the more confident (e.g. Edmund Foster) (*fig.* 133)

Fig. 181 (above left) *Carroll Place, detail of centre bay.* Fig. 182 (above right) *3 Dock Office Row, detail of 'composition' ornamented doorcase.* Figs. 183, 184 (centre left) *11-12 Charlotte Street, details of 'composition' ornamented dado rails.* Fig. 185 (centre right) *183 High Street 'composition' ornamented chimney-piece.* Fig. 186 (bottom left) *7 Charlotte Street, detail of 'composition' ornamented doorcase.* Fig. 187 (bottom right) *76 Lowgate, detail of 'composition' ornamented chimney-piece.*

tempted customers with display pieces in their shop windows. The less affluent toiled in their workshops with little hope of attracting the fashionable. Sometimes they specialised for example as chair makers or oval turners, supplying their standard wares to retailers; others such as Samuel Wallis showed cabinet goods in one window, groceries in the other. Once a firm such as the Walkers had gained the support of a good patron, such as Constable, much of their output consisted of items made to 'special order'. Among the latter were library desks and writing tables (figs. 226, 227) with 'extraordinary wood handles' (these proved to have a wrought iron wire core concealed within carved mahogany handles of conventional profile). The Walkers could also produce attractive inlay (fig. 229) work in the Adam-Chippendale manner. Other 'special orders' include the making of table frames to support the marble and inlaid table tops Constable had bought on his Grand Tours, and furniture designed for the house by a succession of architects.[62] One such brought trouble for the Hargraves. Wyatt had designed the interior furniture and decoration for the Great Drawing Room in 1775 (fig. 122) without troubling himself with precise instructions. He supplied and was paid for, the plates of French glass,[63] and the Hargraves went ahead with all the carving needed for the room (figs. 115, 121) but Constable's table tops were rectangular and Wyatt's supporting frames were segmental and the intended mirror frames were designed en suite. Constable could not sanction cutting up his finest inlaid tops, so he paid off the Hargraves for those carvings 'not used' and brought in the Chippendales to resolve the problems.

Some London architects such as Adam, supplied full size drawings, a practice intended to deny craftsmen scope. Others including Wyatt sent smaller finished drawings which gave craftsmen a greater opportunity for personal invention, as can be seen in any comparison between the original drawings sent to Burton Constable and the outcome. It is not possible to tell by examination which carving is specifically Hull work, nor even that the Hargraves' carving in the Dining and Great Drawing Rooms is by the same hands. The facts are revealed only in the bills, which further tell us for example that Hull carvers had put out their joinery work, and the sawing of mahogany and veneers needed for inlay work, and that some were content with a profit of $12\frac{1}{2}\%$.[64] In 1776, Constable asked one cabinet maker Joseph Foster, to work for him in his London house on minor repairs, de-bugging the beds, etc! 'The time in all was a Bought a fortnight' and Foster's usual charge was two shillings per day plus expenses. For two table frames (fig. 229) and other humbler items he was paid £2. 8s. 0d. in 1774.

Edmund Foster's trade card (fig. 133) reveals a more varied output. He carved and gilded Adamesque oval mirrors for Burton Constable, the Gothick oak case for Snetzler's organ in Beverley Minster, the rococo woodwork on the dais at Beverley Guildhall and a succession of marble church monuments. One, that to John Huntington in Holy Trinity, Hull (fig. 260), he signed 'Ed. Foster scripsit & sc.', a mark of his pleasure in its fine lettering. By the early nineteenth century 'carving' had often become a euphemism for gilded 'composition' (figs. 104, 228) overlaid on a roughly carved wooden frame, the latter made to order by others.

Thomas Ward (1782-1850) and his apprentice Thomas Wilkinson Wallis (1821-1903) worked in every style, as did their chief rival Thomas Brooks (1778-1850) (and, like the Hargraves before them), both worked as well upon ships as upon houses and public buildings. Wallis tells us that external ship carving was rated the lowest, to be done when work was scarce,[65] but the Brooks proudly announced that they had fitted up the state rooms of many Hull built ships, among them the Hull/Hamburg paddle-steamer, the Victoria.[66]

As in the eighteenth century the Constable family liked furniture to 'special order' and Wallis reveals that the gilt and silvered Chinese Dragon Chair (fig. 109) was to a sketch by Lady Marianne Constable, incorporating the family crest.[67] At £31. 10s. 0d. this seems to have been the most expensive chair ever commissioned for Burton Constable. It was but one item in the Regency–Early Victorian refurbishing of the Chinese Room. Thomas Brooks supplied two dragons (fig. 106)[68] for the bay window at a cost of £89. 18s. 0d. Thomas Ward carved a new pagoda cornice inspired by those at Brighton Pavilion, and a pair of bamboo pagoda stands for porcelain (fig. 108). Thomas Meggitt supplied two more such stands, but as befitted a painter (fig. 130), his were japanned with oriental scenes. Meggitt is now remembered for his painting school at which John Ward was a pupil.

Fig. 188 (above left) *Hull Packet 'embellishment' by Thomas Bewick, 1787.* Fig. 189 (above right) *Hull Packet 'embellishment' by Thomas Bewick, 1791.* Fig. 190 (bottom) *High Street, Pease warehouse, interior of 1745 block.*

Fig. 191 (above) *Pease warehouses, 1745, 1760, from Victoria Dock entrance.* Fig. 192 (bottom left) *Castle Street warehouse, weighing scales.* Fig. 193 (bottom right) *Pease warehouse, interior showing grain barrows.*

FIG. 194 (above)   *9-12 King Street, by Joseph Page, c.1771.*   FIG. 195 (below)   *Princes Dock Side from Colonial Chambers to the Waterfront Club.*

For a town of its size, longcase clocks signed by Hull makers are not frequently seen. There are two with conventional cases in Wilberforce House by W. T. Ferrier and G. Pridgin, and another, illustrated here, is signed by William Rust of 20 Market Place (the firm is now in Silver Street) (*fig.* 230), whose mahogany case is a simplification of that shown in plate clxiv of Chippendale's *Director of 1762.*

We know much less about the involvement of Hull craftsmen with the surviving suburban villas, but one at least is worthy of careful study. After the mid century, urban development was counterbalanced by the flight of the wealthiest to those villages that enjoyed pleasant pastoral views with, in some cases, wide ranging vistas across the Humber, for after 1778 it was no longer essential for the merchant to live in close proximity to his business. The movement had begun in the 1760's when the merchant 'aristocracy' liked to enjoy a summer villa. One may think of Sir Henry Etherington at Ferriby and Joseph Pease at Hesslewood. This outward movement was helped by an improvement in both roads and in the comfort of the carriages. J. R. Pease was perhaps exceptional in building both his town and country house at the same time (to be matched by yet another house in the Manchester equivalent of Charlotte Street— Mosley Street. All these were built to the designs of the elder Charles Mountain.

The mid eighteenth century rural counterparts of High Street town mansions are now best represented by Welton Grange and Hull Bank House, usually known as Haworth Hall. The former was built for Richard Bell (Mayor of Hull in 1760 and 1773) c.1750 and has an exceptionally fine interior within the modest compass of its shell, but since it lies well beyond the city boundary we must concentrate upon Haworth Hall, once a seat of the Burton family, then of the Blaydes and finally the Haworth Booths, who unsuccessfully offered the house and park to the city in 1936. The Hall is now the home of the Dunning family, but in the park the great avenues of trees have been replaced by mock neo-Georgian speculative housing. The house however retains its architectural character, shaped by designs of Sir William Chambers (which were first published in 1759 in his *Decorative Part of Civil Architecture*). It is of more than one build, but there is nothing significant that now suggests a date before the 1750's. The pale grey ashlar entrance front (*fig.* 87) is one of the many variations of the Palladian villa theme, popularised not only through the engravings of Colen Campbell and his successors, but by extant examples such as Hotham House at Beverley. The soft texture and colour of the stone work suggests a Nottinghamshire source, perhaps brought from thence by ship via the Trent. The centre is subtly stressed on every storey, the curved pediment being a counterpoise to the repeated horizontals of the rusticated ground floor, there are side sweeps and a bolder cornice to the window over it, and on the top floor each corner of the window architrave is eared. The balustrading beneath the first floor windows hints that this should be the principal floor, overlooking formal gardens, but though there was indeed a splendid avenue of elms stretching westward to the Beverley Road (a motif said to recall for General Burton the battle lines at the battle of the Heights of Abraham), the reception rooms are in fact on the ground floor. This indecision is typical of the mid 1750's, when there was a change in attitude toward garden design, away from formality toward the landscaped park, so that first floor viewing was no longer necessary. (At Everingham Hall c.1757 for example, John Carr first designed a house with its reception rooms on the first floor but just before building began, he gave way to the new mode and brought them down to the floor beneath.) The other three sides of the house have informal elevations, their brickwork harled (*fig.* 85). The Burtons soon sought changes and their unknown architect devised new dining and drawing rooms of greater height than before, a reconstruction that resulted in a remodelling of the Entrance Hall and realignment of the principal staircase (*figs.* 89, 90). The latter with its carved rectangular newel and massive balusters recalls the designs of Abraham Swan, but the new work is, as Colonel R. A. Alec-Smith has pointed out, patently derived from Chambers.[69] His *Civil Architecture* exemplifies good taste cogently argued at every stage, but as a pattern book its themes were not often copied, for they were soon supplanted by those published by Robert and James Adam in their *Works in Architecture*. At Haworth Hall however, chimney-pieces (*figs.* 94, 95, 96) and room cornices echo Chambers' engravings (*figs.* 98, 100), yet the crowding of the exquisitely carved ornament on the principal doorcases (*fig.* 97) and elsewhere makes it unlikely that Chambers himself provided Burton with drawings. Nor would he have countenanced the curious remodelling of the dining room ceiling when the bay was added to that room. The stucco work here is a fusion of the rococo (*fig.* 91) and the neo-classical as can be seen in a comparison of the older acanthus centrepiece with the fluted half patera in the bay. One further link with Chambers deserves mention, the use of palm tree ornaments, here framing the windows of the drawing room (*fig.* 102). In 1761 he had used them for the interior of his Mosque at Kew (a design he had published in 1763) and for the sides of the Coronation Coach (1760-62) but there is too, a design (*fig.* 105) by Thomas Atkinson (c.1729-98) still at Burton Constable, and this comes very close to the one at Haworth Hall. Was Atkinson Burton's architect, or did he select someone from Hull? There were too, minor changes at Haworth Hall — the insertion of a pretty fanlight and new glazing in the entrance door, and the Gothicising of the Library, the former c.1790, the latter perhaps 30 or so years later.

Trinity House

THE TRINITY HOUSE OF HULL probably had its origins in a religious guild set up in 1369, but by the fifteenth century, the guild had taken on a specifically maritime character and its various rights, privileges and obligations were to be confirmed by a succession of royal charters. Not all the income that the House had at its disposal had to be spent exclusively upon charitable works, and this made it possible for money to be spent upon fine buildings and works of art. Indeed during the Georgian period the Trinity House exercised a most important role as patron, and the works they then commissioned now form the most important body of Georgian art and architecture to survive in Hull. As a corporation, in its own right, members of the Board were constantly down in London on House business and as seasoned sea captains they had had an unrivalled opportunity to see the art and architecture of the principal ports of Europe. We know for example that in 1769 Captain Robert Schonswar (Warden in 1788) had played a minor role in delivering John Carr of York's volume of designs for the new hospital of San Antonio in Oporto. The House's own archives record meetings with the town's Members of Parliament, among them such connoisseurs of the arts as William Weddell, Robert Adam's patron at Newby. Should they choose therefore, the Board had easy access to the leading practitioners of their day. The revenues derived from dues upon shipping were only a part of their resources, much of the rest came from the rents of their Whitefriargate estate (*fig.* 134) that had been bequeathed to the House in 1631. This legacy almost certainly included a fragment that still survives embedded in the present Court Room block (*fig.* 140) in the centre of the complex.

As a consistent policy the House has tried to devise a balance between good architecture and rents high enough to cover its needs as a charitable body. In essence this has meant a block by block renewal of their properties fronting Whitefriargate, replacing those that became obsolete or which produced modest rentals, by those with a substantially greater earning capacity. The properties selected for redevelopment were those whose income would show the greatest improvement, not those that fitted into a sequence planned upon architectural principles. Hence by chance, the best buildings were all to be sited well to the left of centre (*figs.* 148, 150). A start was made in 1737[70] but rebuilding continued piecemeal until 1829-30.The tenants were all carefully vetted as to their ability to pay their rents and sureties had to be named to guarantee the rents of tenants who defaulted. Many tenants had direct associations with Trinity House, others were leading craftsmen such as Jeremiah Hargrave (carver), John Waugh (ironsmith), Thomas Towers (bricklayer) and John Fletcher (painter) (*fig.* 129), etc.[71] Tenants frequently called upon the Board to pay for or contribute to such improvements as the fashionable deemed necessary — e.g., marble hearths and slips for chimney-pieces in 1768, printed wallpapers[72] instead of colour wash from 1764, new sashed windows to replace old fashioned casements and bath stoves that gave a brighter fire than those of earlier pattern.

FIG. 196 (opposite)   *Albion Street, north side, 1796.*

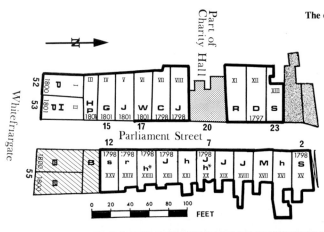

The development of Parliament Street 1796-1801 (numbers as at present)

Key

Builders

C Robert Cross, jr.
M Joseph Hargrave, arch. & carver.
h* Daniel Hopewell, ms.
J George Jackson, bl.
P George Pycock, arch.
R Edward and Thomas Riddell, jr.
s Samuel Stubbs, pl.
W William Walmsley, jr.
No. 10 is by William Upton, pl. and Daniel Hopewell

Developers

B Charles E. Broadley, mer.
D John Daltry, mer.
G James Green, attorney
h Simon Horner, mer.
M Samuel Martin, gent.
S Aistroppe Stovin, attorney

I-XXVIII are the original plot numbers.

 rebuilt   garden ☐ Georgian buildings still standing

Fig. 197 (top) *Plan of Parliament Street.* Fig. 198 (above) *Parliament Street, east side 1796-1800.* Fig. 199 (opposite) *Parliament Street, detail of west side.*

Lots Ground in New Street sold 24th August 1796 by Auction

No.		pr sq. yd.
1	Chs. Broadley	4.5.6
2	,,	4.0.6
3	,,	2.5.6
4	,,	3.3.6
5	,,	2.6.6
6	,,	2.4.6
7	Mr. Cross	2.3.0
8	G. Jackson	2.4.0
9	Mr. Horner	2.3.0
10	Mr. Stovin	2.3.0
11	Mr. Riddell	2.2.6
12	Mr. Daltry	2.2.0
13	Mr. Stovin	2.2.6

No.		pr sq. yd.
14	Mr. Sanderson	1.1(0).0
15	Mr. Stovin	2.2.0
16	Mr. Horner	2.2.6
17	Mr. Martin	2.3.6
19 18	Geo. Jackson	2.6.0

2. (Parliament Street)

No.		pr sq. yd.
18 19	Geo. Jackson	2.5.6
20	D. Hopewell	2.8.0
21	Mr. Horner	2.5.0
22	G. Jackson	2.4.6
23	D. Hopewell	2.2.6
24	R. Richardson	2.3.0
25	Mr. Stubbs	2.3.0
26	C. Broadley	2.10.6
27	,,	5.1.6
28	,,	4.16.0

* H.C.R.O. DDHB 57/204

FIG. 200 (above left) *Kingston Square-John Street;* (left), *Christ Church Schools 1847, by C. Brodrick.* FIG. 201 (above right) *Land of Green Ginger-Manor Street, c.1790.* FIG. 202 (bottom) *York Street, centre house by Appleton Bennison, c.1820.* FIG. 203 (opposite, above left) *Dock Street, houses by the Riddells, c.1792.* FIG. 204 (opposite, centre left) *Baker Street, houses by Appleton Bennison, 1810-24.* FIG. 205 (opposite, bottom left) *Wright Street, houses c.1803-24* FIG. 206 (opposite, right) *Mytongate-Dagger Lane, house by Edward Barker, joiner, 1791.*

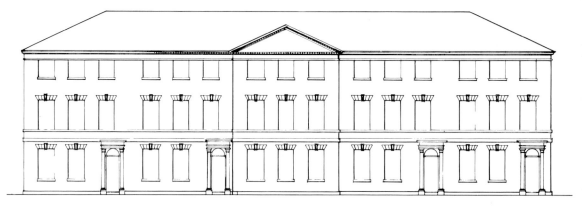

FIG. 207   *Nile Street, south side, houses attributed to Jos. Hargrave, architect, built by Robert Nevis, c.1804, see also fig. 52.*

The climax of this policy was the decision, first discussed in 1791, to replace a block of old property by a splendid new Inn and two handsome houses (*figs*. 148, 152, 154, 155), but by the time the notice given to existing tenants had expired, England had had two years at war with France and the rapid growth in Hull's prosperity as a port had been severely checked. Nothing daunted, the Board pressed on with the project, letting the houses in 1796. The Inn, to be called the Neptune (now Messrs. Boots) was advertised in 1795. The expected rent was too high for difficult times and the Neptune quickly proved a commercial failure. Thereafter the board became more cautious and did nothing in Whitefriargate for thirty years, when a group of five shops and houses were built as a centrepiece for the western half of the frontage (*figs*. 159, 161) and finally in 1829 the Board decided to rebuild everything east of the Neptune, with a Bank in the centre (now Messrs. Woolworths) and four shops and houses on either side (*figs*. 136, 150). In all, this renewal of the southern side of Whitefriargate had taken ninety three years. In the interim there had been a notable shift in the pattern of urban use, for what had, for most of the time been a replacement of modest houses, stables, workshops and shops by better houses and shops had become, by the 1820's, one of shopkeepers who no longer wished to occupy the domestic part of the building they rented, and one in which there was a trend toward professional or office use, with fewer and fewer now caring to live even in a fashionable street in the Old Town. Thus from the 1820's the Board came under constant pressure to allow shopkeepers to extend their shops in depth into the domestic quarters, and to allow subletting of the unwanted upper floors. The Board could not always resist requests of the first type, but stood firmly against the second, because of the difficulty of effective control over subtenants. The outcome has been the survival of at least the shells of the Georgian buildings, because it no longer paid the Board to demolish and rebuild — only to renew the shopfronts or redecorate the upper floors with stucco (*fig*. 161).

Prior to the building of the Neptune, the Whitefriargate houses were conventional three bay fronts that differed only in detail (*fig*. 148) in accordance with current fashion. There seems to have been no separate provision of shop fronts as such, but in both of the blocks built in the 1820's the shop front is the predominant element, and as in Nash's Regent Street, pilasters, pediments, sculpture and other decorative devices were used to create a palatial effect (*fig*. 157).

George Pycock's design for the Neptune block emphasised the splendid ballroom within (*fig*. 152). He gave the latter arched windows, the central one being a Venetian (*figs*. 154, 155). The round arched theme was repeated in the end pavilions to bind the composition together vertically, but the arches here supported pediments (*fig*. 155). The topmost floor was redesigned during the course of building, an alteration that reduces the aesthetic value of the pediments. The flanking houses were simply designed, though taller than their existing neighbours. To the west, the five houses of 1826 were given greater prominence by a range of antae and a corresponding sub-division of the attic floor (*fig*. 161) but the composition, even when designed, had its ground floor wholly taken up by shop fronts (*fig*. 159). The architect was probably Charles Mountain junior, its builders certainly F. and J. Appleyard. Three years later, the Board sought architects for the rebuilding of the site, Nos. 1-10.

Fig. 208 (above left)   *6-8 Pier Street built for Edward Rheam, c.1824, demolished 1978.*   Fig. 209 (above centre)   *2 York Street, doorcase by A. Bennison, c.1820.*   Fig. 210 (above right)   *17 Pier Street, doorcase by W. Westerdale, c.1817.*   Fig. 211 (bottom left)   *24-28 Queen Street, c.1803.*   Fig. 212 (bottom right)   *17 Pier Street, painted dummy windows, c.1817.*

Figs. 213, 214, 215, 216 (opposite) *Theatre Royal. Four sketches by Thomas Willis of his scenery for the theatre, 1816.* Fig. 217 (above left) *Humber Street, Theatre Royal, C. Mountain, Jnr., architect, 1809, from Greenwood.* Fig. 218 (above right) *Dr. John Alderson, Thomas Earle, sculptor, now in City Hall.* Fig. 219 (bottom) *Hull Royal Infirmary, entrance hall and staircase, George Pycock, architect, 1783.*

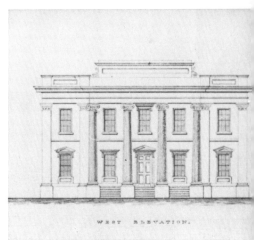

WEST ELEVATION.

FIG. 220 (above left) *Kingston Square, Public Rooms as proposed by R. H. Sharp, 1827, not executed.* FIG. 221 (above right) *Kingston Square, Public Rooms as proposed by C. Mountain, Jnr., 1829, nearly as executed.* FIG. 222 (bottom) *Charles Street, west side, early 1800's.* FIG. 223 (opposite, above) *Jarratt Street and Worship Street, c.1803-06.* FIG. 224 (opposite, bottom) *Charles Street, east side, mostly 1820-30.*

George Jackson junior suggested an evenly spaced grouping of four identical pavilions with an Ionic colonnade for the Bank in the centre, and plain windows for the houses on either side (*fig.* 157). It is possible that the Board felt that Jackson's pavilions might clash with those of the Neptune, so they accepted Mountain's design with its pilastered and pedimented centrepiece (*figs.* 136, 150) and reticent pavilions. The sculptured pediment by Thomas Earle was the third such feature to be commissioned by the Board (*figs.* 136, 158). Within a few years, and constantly thereafter, the Board was being asked to substitute large sheets of plate glass for panes of smaller size, but since it was not expected that all tenants would want plate glass, in 1837 the Board ordered the acquisition of 'bent squares' for the older shop fronts, in case they should prove difficult to obtain.

Of interiors only the 'Neptune Inn' now retains any high architectural value (*fig.* 152). When opened, its many fine rooms were fitted with handsome furniture, including 22 four poster beds with 'dimity chintz and moreen' hangings, '156 mahogany, walnut, cherry tree and painted chairs', mahogany dining, tea and Pembroke tables, etc.[73]

The redevelopment of the remaining properties bounded by Trinity House Lane, Posterngate and Prince's Dockside was equally long drawn out. The House itself was rebuilt between 1753 and 59 (*figs.* 135, 138) with Jeremiah Hargrave as possible architect, a project that allowed a modest re-alignment of the junction of Trinity House Lane and Posterngate. At the same time, builders encased the original core in red stock brick with stone facings in the same style (*fig.* 140). The nine bay front is still dominated by Hargrave's sculptured pediment (*fig.* 135), for which he was paid £105 in 1758 and a further £25 in 1759, but the original balance between brick and stone was to be changed when the building was stuccoed in 1828, a similar finish being given to the much plainer façade in Posterngate. To harmonise these two fronts, stucco window-frames and other details had to be added to the latter.

To minimise the nuisance of noise, the windows of the street front light only the corridors, the pensioners' windows face on to the inner court. By 1764 the House's funds had not merely recovered, they were steadily increasing as the port's trade flourished, and in that year the Board commissioned George Schonswar (joiner) and Thomas Towers (bricklayer) to build three new houses in Posterngate (*figs.* 149, 162-4). No. 34, the smallest, was let to the Warden's clerk, No. 33 was let to John Banks (twice Mayor) and No. 32 to Mrs. Mace, the latter both for £18. The contractors had however displeased the Board, who resolved not to employ them again upon the House's business. By chance the centre house (No. 33) has survived with little internal alteration, and its handsome staircases (*figs.* 163, 164) are the only wooden ones of the mid-Georgian period, whose design and authorship are known. Schonswar's principal staircase is of the usual Hull pattern, but the secondary staircase (*fig.* 163) is one of the now rare examples of the Chinese Chippendale style. To save space it runs from an inner corner of the first floor landing to the roof, with the same basic pattern of balustrade throughout. Schonswar presumably possessed or had seen a copy of William and John Halfpenny's *Rural Architecture in the Chinese Taste*, for plates 2, 16 and 50 (of the second edition 1752) show the balustrade either as a fencing panel or within a staircase. For some reason only the top-most panel at Posterngate identically repeats Halfpenny's model, the rest have a minor bar omitted.

Joseph Page was paid £3 for stucco work here — perhaps for the Venetian window? (*fig.* 164).

No less interesting, the authors discovered a panel of Adamesque wallpaper lining the wall within a Georgian cupboard (*fig.* 162 and half title), which is likely to have been put on by Alderman John Bank's during his tenancy of 1765-97, most likely when he became Mayor in 1789 as it is recorded that in this year his house was redecorated. The background of the paper is a soft cream with the pattern printed in two shades of grey, its cost probably $4\frac{1}{2}$d. per yard.[74]

In 1772 the House embarked upon a much grander project — the building of a new Chapel (*fig.* 143) and the reconstruction of the reception rooms now called the Court Room and the Council

FIG. 225 (opposite, above left)   *94 George Street, inlaid staircase whorl.*   FIG. 226 (opposite, above right)   *Burton Constable, detail of inlaid writing desk by Thomas Walker, 1779.*   FIG. 227 (opposite, centre left)   *Burton Constable, bureau by Thomas and Robert Walker, 1791-92.*   FIG. 228 (opposite, centre right)   *Burton Constable, Vine Table by Thomas Brooks, 1844.*   FIG. 229 (opposite, bottom left)   *Burton Constable, side table by Jos. Foster after a design by Lightoler, 1774.*   FIG. 230 (opposite, bottom right)   *Burton Constable, clock by William Rust.*

Chamber. They sought advice upon both from Sir William Chambers,[75] the Surveyor General who was almost certainly related to both Dr. Chambers and to Thomas Chambers (a Master Warden and one of the Board). In the end Chambers was only responsible for the Chapel. His first design for the facade was too plain and the Board wrote to ask him to give the front greater consequence since it faced the street. The outcome was a triangular pediment supported by two tall Doric pilasters and a length of architrave and frieze. The east window was thus a narrow rectangle, and for this the Board asked William Peckitt to design suitable stained glass. They paid him £5 5s. 0d. for his trouble, but did not order the glass because Sir William thought that any such glass was inappropriate for a classical setting. Chambers was also asked for designs for the altar (*fig.* 83), pulpit and other fittings (but only the altar survived the demolition of the Chapel in c.1843). Nearly a decade later Mountain and Riddell added a small almshouse and Marine School to the north of the Chapel (*fig.* 143) with a pediment to match the latter. Chambers probably never came to Hull during the work, but was rewarded by a present of the best ale and some Yorkshire hams. The advice he gave on the new rooms is not recorded, but he was much involved with a commission to secure a portrait of the King. He recommended the Scottish painter, Sir George Chalmers, just possibly because the two were distantly related (for Chambers is an anglicisation of Chalmers). Sir George proved to be dilatory, but in the end the Board, after appeals to Chambers and others, managed to get the King's personal approbation of the portrait. Chalmers was paid £52 10s. 0d., while the picture framer charged a further £23 (*fig.* 141).

FIG. 231 (opposite) *35 Blanket Row, c.1801.* FIG. 232 (above) *Hessle Road, detail of Vauxhall Tavern, c.1814.*
FIG. 233 (bottom) *35 Beverley Road, built as two houses.*

The remodelling of the Court and Council rooms was given to Joseph Page in 1773.[76] He raised the external walls nine feet (*fig.* 140) and this gave him enough room for a splendid coved ceiling (*fig.* 139) perhaps the first in Hull to be nominally in the Adam style, though with its ovals of foliage, it is closer to the manner of James Wyatt, Adam's strongest rival. The east wall is dominated by two elegant Venetian windows (*fig.* 142), a motif of the Kent school, though the details of the capitals and bases betray the later date. Kent had intended Venetian openings for the dining room at Houghton, a scheme engraved in Ware's *Inigo Jones* (plate xxxv), but that version was not executed. In the 1750's Carr revived the theme for the great Dining Room at Heath Hall near Wakefield, though there it is overlaid by rococo ornament. Page's decoration is not only neo-classical, but is carefully linked with both the doorcases and the chimney-piece (*fig.* 145). The ceiling of the bay has the fan motif that Charles Mountain was to use in the 1780's at 11-15 Charlotte Street and perhaps elsewhere. Page's chimney-piece is of white marble with brightly coloured inlays of scagliola, perhaps by Domenico Bartoli. Chalmer's portrait neatly fits the panel above (*fig.* 146, 147). Page seems to have been content to leave the irregularity of the room shape undisturbed, though he could not resist the temptation to add triangular corner pieces above the blind arches of the Venetian windows, the sort of detail to which a leading London architect would have given greater thought. Page's interior of the adjacent Council Chamber was modified by the insertion of new windows in the 1840's and yet again after a fire in the 1920's when the present Adam style ceiling replaced that of Page [he had devised one of a central chandelier patera framed within a circular decorative border which criss-crossed a larger rectangle that followed the edge of the ceiling]. The present black and gold chimney-piece dates from the 1840's.

Early Victorian alterations involved a new oak staircase and landing between the Court and Council Rooms, an approach that gives no hint of either the antiquity of the building or of the Georgian splendour of the Court Room. The present chandelier (*fig.* 141) was given to the House in 1821 and according to a tradition repeated by Greenwood in 1835, it came from Carlton House. To the north of the older rooms, the House added the Museum and Reading Rooms— the latter a top-lit oval, and at the same time built the third Chapel, that of Chambers having proved too small and incapable of worthwhile enlargement. The House decided to sacrifice a part of their garden, so that, if necessary, the nave could be extended westward. H. F. Lockwood submitted his designs in 1839[77] though the chapel was not finished until 1843. Externally the building is a simple rectangle, with pediment and Greek Corinthian pilasters (*fig.* 144) facing east, and a tall porch framed by antae to the west. Over the porch one can see one of the three lunettes that light the interior. Within, Lockwood showed ingenuity, with a strongly axial plan yet with a central cube ceiled by a ribbed dome (*fig.* 153). To the east the altar was placed within a coffered apse balanced at the western end by a coffered barrel vault of equal span. The Order is Corinthian with nautical motifs in the capitals, and veined white marble pilasters. The dado and the two engaged columns in the apse are of brown Ashford marble, and more marble was used for the inlaid floor. The oak box pews and pulpit also survive thus making the Chapel a rare example of a rich Early Victorian interior.

Mr. John Barling drew our attention to Lockwood's contract drawings which still exist in the archives of the Surveyor's department and it was interesting to see how many changes of detail were made during the progress of the work. For example a single large pulpit was substituted for two smaller symmetrical ones shown in the drawing.

The pressure of work that had accumulated during the 1830's and 40's prompted the Board to change its policy of relying upon outside architects such as Charles Mountain junior who had designed the new almshouses in Posterngate (1828) and Carr Lane (1834) (*fig.* 156) and John Earle, who was responsible for the Ferries Hospital (1822) (*figs.* 137, 195) on Princes Dockside. Instead they appointed surveyors such as William Foale,[78] among whose early designs were those for the Victoria Almshouses (1842), the new Post Office in a courtyard off Whitefriargate, the new offices of the House (in Trinity House Lane, 1844) on the site of Sir William Chambers Chapel, Colonial Chambers (1846) (*fig.* 195), etc. As surveyor, Foale also kept a watchful eye upon those parts of the Trinity House estate that were ripe for development, for example the Closes south of Spring Bank and he may well have acted as architect for neighbouring owners by designing a group of houses in Park Street (*figs.* 270, 271, 273, 274-7).

Neo-Classicism

IN THE LAST QUARTER of the century there were numerous changes in the cultural life of Hull that matched the tendency toward greater elegance in daily life. In architecture, Joseph Page, the Riddells and the elder Mountain worked in the Adam style, and even modest houses could now have chimney-pieces with Adamesque ornament in 'composition'. The Hull Subscription Library was founded in 1775 (though its headquarters designed by Joseph Hargrave were not built until 1801), and, in the field of art, painters in water colour and oil began to find a market for their paintings, now most obviously those used for the illustration of Hadley's and Tickell's *Histories of Hull*. Engravers too found a growing demand, though the most brilliant, Robert Thew, had to move to London where he worked upon Boydell's 'Shakespeare'. Thew's best known engravings are the map of Hull published 1784 and the two views of the new Dock. (He had started life as a cooper.) There were too, the delicate watercolours of Benjamin Gale, and a succession of oil painters produced river, town and seascapes, culminating in the work of John Ward (1798-1849) (*fig.* 268). This new mood is perhaps best summarised in the embellishments engraved for the *Hull Packet* in 1787 and 1791 (*figs.* 188, 189). Both were cut by Thomas Bewick (1753-1828) of Newcastle to match the selfconscious choice of fine type bought from Caslon, the King's Type-founder. That engraved for George Prince shows a prosperous 'Kingstonia', seated among cargo, with crowded shipping and the town's arms to the left and a view of the citadel from the Humber to the right. The embellishment ordered by Thomas Lee is a chaste oval bearing the town's arms framed by branches of palm and olive (*figs.* 188, 189).[79] The first was belated Baroque, the second wholly neo-classical, but both styles retained adherents in Hull, for example the monument by Earle at Hemingbrough or the trade card of Meggitt and Son (*fig.* 130) are Baroque, and as at York, Adamesque chimney-pieces were still installed in the 1820's and 1830's such as that at 87 Beverley Road, and one (found recently) in Spring Street.

FIG. 234 *Minerva Terrace, c.1830.*

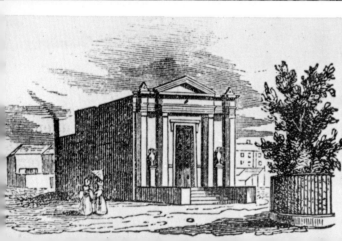

The neo-classical style was introduced quite early into Hull — at Haworth Hall (*figs.* 94-101), in the Chambers manner, and at Trinity House (*figs.* 139-142) in the version favoured by Robert Adam and James Wyatt, but the underlying framework was still Palladian, softened by an overlay of exquisite ornament, such as that applied (perhaps by Charles Mountain sen.) in Carroll Place (*fig.* 181). The new houses were taller and had larger sites. When newly built, every aspect of interior decoration could be harmonised — the wallpapers, curtains and upholstery, the furniture, china, silverware and glass, all linked by the same vocabulary of ornament and by a carefully matched and brilliant colour scheme. Shorn of these accessories the now whitened ceilings and bare painted walls lack the impact of earlier carving and panelling now that most buildings of the period have been converted to commercial or industrial use. The Adamesque phase lasted until the 1790's and culminated in Pycock's great Banqueting Room (*fig.* 152) at the Neptune, with less spectacular but still charming ceilings at 11-15 Charlotte Street (*fig.* 178), the Chapel of the Charterhouse (*fig.* 167) or in the former Branch Bank of England house, 50 Saltshouse Lane. The Adam style seemed an easy one to imitate, for its range of ornament was simple to grasp and became cheap and easy to manufacture in cast plaster, 'composition', Coade stone and cast metals such as lead, brass and iron. Adam, unlike most of his imitators, knew the value of subtle contrast between adjacent similar ornament, of carefully devised frames to show off the delicacy of the ornament within them, and of devices such as leaving motifs at the edges of a ceiling incomplete so that the mind's eye finished them, thus apparently enlarging the ceiling. The Charlotte Street ceilings were cast from a limited range of moulds— an umbrella fan, small ivy-like leaves arranged in loops or garlands, a border of honeysuckle flowers or tiny leaves, and a centrepiece of thin overlapping foliage. Both plain and enriched cornices were frequently given a little wavy motif at the junction with the wall, best described as a 'pie-crust frill', examples of which abound in George Street, Dock Street and Albion Street. Adam's 'rainceau', a wiry spiral overlaid with curls of acanthus leaves was used indoors and out— on ceilings, chimney-pieces, dado rails, on the over door and external pediments of Charlotte Street (*figs.* 176, 177) and on chimney-piece friezes in Parliament Street. The same feeling for elegance resulted in a variety of enriched capitals for the doorcases of Parliament Street, the cornices of the houses in George Street or Dock Street and in the inlaid fans or flowers done in contrasting veneers in the stair foot spirals of houses in Albion Street (e.g. No. 22 Albion Street or 94 George Street) (*fig.* 225). As before, stair balusters were usually turned out of thin slender stuff sometimes of mahogany, such as Mountain designed for 12 Charlotte Street or Hesslewood both of 1783, and both houses were also furnished with splendidly figured and polished mahogany doors.[80] The same wood was also used for simpler stair balusters of square or rectangular section, with two sides left plain, the other grooved with a moulding plane as formerly in Great Union Street. The introduction of an area in front of the houses in the New Town and the suburbs created work for the ironfounder, who employed wood carvers to make the models for balusters, newel posts, fanlights, finials, railing stays and shoe scrapers. In the 1780's these were mostly of simple form but by the early nineteenth century they were more richly modelled and, because they were easily reproduced these late Georgian patterns remained current until at least the 1840's (*figs.* 246-251). The popularity of the cast iron balcony dates here from the 1780's, its earlier name 'window guard' hinting at its real purpose (*figs.* 239-242). When cotton manufacture rapidly expanded as a result of progressive mechanisation, it became fashionable to devise voluminous window draperies which, in older rooms, masked too much window glass. Now windows often stretched from floor to ceiling and were framed by more widely splayed fixed shutter panels that allowed the curtains to fall in front of them rather than the window panes. The advent of the balcony also reminds us that the cruder habits such as the committing of 'nuisance' or the emptying of chamber pots into the street or carrying out hazardous trade operations or slaughtering beasts were by now largely banished, at least from the more respectable streets, and the various Hull Improvement Acts also had clauses to curtail the encroachment of door steps and shop windows and to hasten the supply of downspouts to carry away rain water. There developed two patterns of lead rainwater head, the bowl and the trumpet (as at the Neptune, where they were made by David Wharam), sometimes

FIGS. 235 (opposite, above left), 236 (opposite, bottom left) *Kingston Square, Hull Medical School, entrance door and Greenwood's View, 1833. H. R. Abraham, architect.* FIG. 237 (opposite, above right) *55 Spring Bank, detail of façade.* FIG. 238 (opposite, bottom right) *89 Beverley Road, terrace house of c.1830.*

plainly moulded, but as frequently with a band of fluting. Both patterns remained in use until the 1840's. They are rarely dated, and in this, Hull practice differs from that in most towns.

Elegance and refinement were not confined to houses, for the Charterhouse, rebuilt in 1779-80, probably to the designs of Joseph Hargrave, has a bold domed porch, wide pediment and generous cupola externally and a handsome chapel within. The latter has a carved Adamesque doorcase, stucco ceiling and a splendid neo-classical mahogany pulpit and tester (*figs.* 165, 167) entered from a door let into the wall in the continental rather than the English manner. Hargrave was paid £5 5s. in 1778-9, i.e. before his services as a carver could be needed, and he signs the engraving of the Charterhouse in Hadley's *History of Hull*, 'Jos. Hargrave, Architt & delint.'

The new Infirmary, designed by George Pycock in 1783 was more coldly handsome, because its size dwarfed the domestic scale of its entrance porch and the Venetian and lunette windows over it. Within, the hall was given a plain classical wooden chimney-piece[82] and from here the great staircase could be seen between the screen of Doric columns (*fig.* 219).

Even structures as utilitarian as factories had their quota of pediments and other genteel features composed with precise symmetry. In the Boulton and Watt papers there are finely drawn designs for the steam corn mill in Wincolmlee of Messrs. Thompson & Baxter of 1787-88 (*fig.* 245),[83] and a token penny issued by the lead manufacturer, John Picard, shows the front of his leadworks just north of Whitefriargate (*fig.* 246). It would be easier to draw the parallel between the steam mill and a house if the bottom storey had been sunk within an area and the entrance door placed in the storey above.

Until the 'Adam' period, probably all the decorative motifs had been made in Hull, but a little Coade stone had been brought in from London. A plaque in this artificial stone can be seen in the 'Citadel Ruin' in East Park. There was the more considerable use of another Georgian synthetic, 'composition'. Typically it was made from wood powder, whiting and glue — raw materials that were cheap, and readily available. The 'composition' was firmly pressed into carefully prepared moulds, the motifs could then be sold singly, by the foot or dozen, or in sets ready glued on to a pine backing for use as chimney-piece or doorcase friezes (*figs.* 182-187), cornices or pilasters. In 1795, William Settle,[84] a Hull builder, advertised that he sold the 'composition' made by the Wolstenholmes of York claiming that their product was 70% better than that made locally. Both Coade stone and 'composition' began to be widely marketed in 1760's and in the next two decades they were used in the finest town and country houses, but there their very cheapness told against them. By the 1790's most towns had streets such as Parliament Street or Nile Street wholly decorated with 'composition' ornament. The original moulds had to be carved with exquisite delicacy but layers of paint now blur the crisp detail they produced. Designers used their Adam vocabulary enlivened with figure plaques based upon currently popular paintings or engravings. For example there is a panel of 'The Dance' after Henry Bunbury in Parliament Street, and others after engravings of George Richardson in Maisters House and Hesslewood.

By the 1790's too, both the Coades, and 'composition' ornament makers, had published illustrated catalogues of their wares. A Coade catalogue can be seen in the Soane Museum and an untitled catalogue of 'composition' motifs exists in the Henry Francis Du Pont Winterthur Museum at Winterthur, U.S.A. From the latter we have learnt that the typical Parliament Street chimney-piece would have cost 17s. to £1 10s. as complete sets. Inevitably the introduction of such materials must affect the Hull style and bring it closer to that prevailing elsewhere. Thus the doorway at 3 Dock Office Row (*fig.* 182) could easily be found in York, Manchester and Liverpool, there being nothing to indicate that it is made in Hull. At the Lawson-Haworth houses 202/203 High Street one chimney-piece (*fig.* 168) had a handsome frieze with just the controlled 'movement' and variety that Adam had advocated in his 'Works'. That formerly at 183 High Street (*fig.* 185) as well as the one still extant at 76 Lowgate (*fig.* 187) would look equally well in the bedroom of a country house. It is when the motifs are over loaded or reduced to too small a scale that one must question the taste of manufacturer and

CAST IRON BALCONIES
FIG. 239 (opposite, above left) *Parliament Street, c.1796-1800.* FIG. 240 (opposite, above right) *10 Charlotte Street. c.1793* FIG. 241 (opposite, centre) *81 Beverley Road, c.1830* FIG. 242 (opposite bottom) *4 Humber Place, c.1850.*

user alike, but this criticism is not new, for the Roman writer of the first century A.D., Vitruvius had commented on the misuse of painted ornament of an architectural character — just the sort of ornament whose discovery at Pompeii and Herculaneum proved so influential upon the Adam style. In Hull two examples may be quoted of the Herculaneum influence — the marble drawing room chimney-piece at Hesslewood (*fig.* 258) and, in a quite different context, the trade card of Richard Smithson,[85] a bookbinder of 16 Parliament Street. The chimney-piece has two 'Herculaneum' nymphs flanking an 'Antique' panel of Friendship consoling Affliction, the trade card shows a group of winged cherubs hard at work upon bookbinding in an otherwise Gothic setting.

Not one Georgian or Regency shop front now survives intact in Hull, but Hargrave's view of the Market Place published in 1788 shows that that street was lined with bow windows. The Trinity House Vote Books record that a double fronted one put up in Lowgate in 1792, was made by Mann and Beaumont for £20. That still at Blanket Row[91] has lost its sash bars but is otherwise complete, but the one at the corner of Grimston Street and Garden Street (1829) has its pilasters whose hooked tops were a characteristic feature of so many of the doorcases in English Street and its vicinity.[92]

A reaction to surface prettiness was inevitable. Some might turn toward the Gothic, though few in Hull were to do so except for

FIG. 243 (above) *Burton Constable, 'Tulip Shade' supplied by Thomas Purdon of Whitefriargate, 1837.* FIG. 244 (centre) *Haworth Hall, brass door fittings, c.1760-70.* FIG. 245 (bottom left) *Wincolmlee, elevation of Thompson & Baxter's Steam Corn Mill, 1788 (redrawn).* FIG. 246 (bottom right) *Hull Lead Works penny token of John Picard, 1812, showing Picard's factory off Whitefriargate.*

CAST IRON WORK, c.1820-45.
FIG. 247 (above left)   *55 Spring Bank.*   FIG. 248 (above centre)   *Canton Place, Anlaby Road.*   FIG. 249a (above right)
FIG. 249b (bottom left top)   *Kingston Square.*   FIG. 250 (bottom left below)   *High Street.*   FIG. 251 (bottom centre)
Nelson Terrace, Park Street.   FIG. 252 (bottom right)   *Georgian lamp post, Bankside, Sculcoates, c.1825.*

Fig. 253 (opposite, above) *37 High Street, 1829.* Fig. 254 (opposite, bottom) *Dock Office Row, former Dock Office (now Oriental Buildings), c.1820.* Fig. 255 (above left, 256 (above right) *Nelson Street Pilot Office staircase and Board Room chimney-piece, 1819-20.* Fig. 257 (bottom left) *Dock Office Row, former Dock Office oval staircase, 1820.* Fig. 258 (bottom right) *Hesslewood, detail of chimney-piece showing Herculaneum nymph.*

FIG. 259 (above left)   *New St. Mary's Church, Sculcoates — re-used columns from 1761 church.*   FIG. 260 (above right top)   *Holy Trinity Church: Huntington monument by Edmund Foster, c.1790.*   FIG. 261 (above right)   *Henry Maister monument, c.1699.*   FIG. 262 (centre left)   *Detail of Nathaniel Maister monument, c.1783.*   FIG. 263 (bottom left)   *203 High Street, detail of 'composition' chimney-piece (c.f. fig. 262)*   FIG. 264 (bottom right)   *Drypool churchyard, detail of mariner's gravestone.*

church building and the occasional college. The alternative was to replace the Roman by the Greek, using stucco instead of exposed brick, and, by taking advantage of the canals, to bring in great blocks of West Riding building stone for the sturdy Greek Doric columns of porticoes and for the monumental staircases of public buildings.

Regency

THE FIRST HINTS OF THE REGENCY STYLE might be traced back to the 1780's in the work of James Wyatt and Henry Holland, to be followed in the next decade by the startlingly original designs of Sir John Soane, but it would be difficult to pin-point any Hull parallel before the 1820's, by which time the style had spread throughout England, and most large towns had their prac-titioners in the Greek Revival manner. In Hull it was to be Charles Mountain the younger (1773-1839) who took over his father's practice after the latter's death in 1805, though there is nothing for example in the new Theatre Royal to betray a date of 1809-10, for Mountain repeated the blind arcading device his father had used in the Pease House of 1783. Though this theatre was destroyed by fire in 1859, a book of scenery designs for the stage consisting of monochrome watercolour sketches does sur-vive, dating from 1816 (now in the Museum) (*figs*. 176, 217). The designs are similarly con-servative and show either classical landscapes of the sort long used by portrait painters as back-grounds for 'Grand Tourists', or a series of staircases of barely medieval or wildly Piranesian character, and a landscape of a temple fragment perched above the tumbling waters of a gorge (*figs*. 213-216). The painter, Thomas Willis, does not appear in the Hull directory, unlike the author of another group of stage scenery, William Binks. The rolls of back-drops (which were recently discovered by Mrs. Gay Chichester-Constable) are survivors from the private theatre at Burton Constable, a ven-ture of Lady Marianne Clifford Constable, who

FIG. 265 (above) *Former Scott Street Chapel.*
FIG. 266 (below) *St. Charles' Church, Jarratt Street, John Earle 1829, J. J. Scoles 1835 and Smith, Brodrick & Lowther, 1894.*

brought in both amateurs and professionals from the Hull theatres. Some scenes are typical of the English watercolours of the 1820's and 30's depicting continental scenery of northern Europe, but the conservatory interior here shown has a likely date of 1840's, i.e. when the Great Stove at Chatsworth and the Palm House at Kew were new (fig. 269).

Subsequently Mountain was much employed by Trinity House to design and build the almshouses in Posterngate and Carr Lane and on the final stages of the redevelopment of Whitefriargate (figs. 150, 156). All was firmly Greek Revival as was his new front to Beverley Guildhall of 1832. In his Trinity House work, Mountain repeated the bracketted window cornices to be found in the 1753 block (as William Foale was also to do in 1848 when designing a range of almshouses to be built behind Mountain's). His competitors could be less cautious. They included Appleton Bennison, the younger Pycock (d.1815), George Jackson, David Thorp, William Hutchinson (1779-1869) and from further afield, York architects such as Peter Atkinson (1776-1843) or Richard Hey Sharp (1793-1853) his pupil, John Clark from Leeds (d.1857) and from London, H. R. Abraham (1774-1850) and David Laing (1774-1856). Atkinson designed a charming villa at Bilton and church at Sproatley and Sharp's splendid schemes for the new Public Rooms were, in the end passed over in favour of those of Mountain (figs. 220, 221).[86] Clark was responsible for the Wilberforce column in 1834, but the theme was by then a familiar one. Henry R. Abraham's Medical School (figs. 235, 236) faces the Public Rooms in Kingston Square though because of its modest scale, its facade tends to be overlooked. In fact the detailing is worth study though the Greek amphorae shown in Greenwood's engraving have long gone. The sloping sides of the entrance door imitate those of Greek temples — a feature much exaggerated in the illustration because of the now cramped viewpoint. In 1815 David Laing had surveyed the Neptune Inn in his capacity as Surveyor to the Customs prior to the lease of that building as the Customs House, but his other commission in Hull, for a new block of property in Dock Office Row seems not to have been built. These but few incursions from outside left the field in the hands of local men, but Mountain went to live in Malton in 1835 before going to Wakefield (where he died in 1839) but by that date Henry Francis Lockwood (1811-1878) had begun practice in Hull, aided for a time by his pupil Cuthbert Brodrick (1821-1906). In 1832 Lockwood was being employed on minor works at Burton Constable, such as the new Jacobean conservatory which was added to the south western corner of the house,[87] followed in 1837 by Kingston College, Beverley Road, an essay in the Gothic style. Two years later he was asked to design a new chapel for Trinity House (figs. 144, 153), whose success may have prompted others to employ him as a confident exponent of classical architecture. In Hull one may cite the chapels of Albion Street and Great Thornton Street. In the interim he encased and remodelled Pycock's Infirmary of 1783, adding stucco to the brick walls and a Greek Corinthian order for the portico and end pavilions. (That this was a cosmetic operation could be seen by comparing Lockwood's rectangular window on the top floor externally and Pycock's tripartite lunette internally.) If the younger Mountain was a provincial counterpart to Sir Robert Smirke in his handling of the Doric Order, so Lockwood may be compared to the brilliant Charles Robert Cockerell (1788-1863) not least in the way that both men combined a refinement typically Greek with a planning and spatial quality that was Baroque, in inspiration. By the late 1830's the classical style had, for many, run its course, but in Hull Lockwood not only gave it a further lease of life, but inspired Brodrick to continue working in his style. Lockwood gave the Albion Street Chapel a monumental Greek Doric portico that was much more convincing than Mountain's at the Master Mariner's almshouse, and his front to Great Thornton Street Chapel, also of 1842, was worthy of a better site. The centrepiece was an eight columned Corinthian portico flanked by open Doric colonnades and pedimented end pavilions. To give his composition greater force in the long street, the whole complex was raised upon a podium, with a broad flight of steps in the middle. The composition echoes, though more grandly, Nicholas Revett's church in the park at Ayot St. Lawrence, Hertfordshire (built in 1778). Just as one instance of the architect's careful attention to detail — the bottom newel for the gallery staircase in the Chapel of Trinity House is an elegant cast iron standard modelled upon an Antique Roman candelabrum. Lockwood's Gothic work was competent but unexciting by comparison.

FIG. 267 (opposite, above & below)   *Coltman Street, typical Greek Revival houses of the earlier 1840's.*

Fig. 268   *John Ward (c.1798-1849), Hull from the Humber (Minerva Terrace* (see fig. 234), *Nelson Street and Queen Street).*

As elsewhere at this time, the majority of houses were the work of speculative builders, who in order to attract buyers, tricked out their houses with such ornament as they believed their clients would expect. The doorway was the obvious place to decorate, even in the humblest houses — a few simple mouldings or a fashionable fanlight were enough here. When these would not suffice, a carved stone window head, a full architrave, a moulded wood or stucco cornice, or a few shallow pilasters as in 89 Spring Bank or Beverley Road would attract the eye. Tall columned porches were even more respectable — some of but slight projection as in Spring Street, other of the boldness for example of 215 Anlaby road (*fig*. 283). The latter, of the early 1840's, is perhaps by George Jackson jun. A full portico such as that shown in old photographs of the former country villa, Newington Hall, was an overt luxury that was reminiscent of Cheltenham and it may indeed have been a work of John Buonarotti Papworth (1775-1847) [Papworth's drawing for the gate-piers for Newington is dated 1843 and it is unlikely that a London architect would have been called upon to design only gate-piers]. Fortunately some of the other long demolished Regency villas were recorded in the watercolours of F. S. Smith.

Internally the reception rooms and principal bedrooms would have wide moulded door archi-traves, plain or enriched plaster cornices (*figs*. 4, 274-277) and chimney-pieces in wood, stone or marble. By far the commonest new pattern for doorcases and chimney-pieces was a band of simple mouldings set within a plain raised frame and with square sunk panels at the upper corners — the latter ornamented with a turned patera or a carved or 'composition' Grecian flower. The mantel shelf was usually a plain slab with small quadrants at the corners. Such chimney-pieces were often painted in simulation of more expensive materials, while those of marble were often of white, or white and dove grey or fossil marble, their smooth surfaces highly polished in maximum contrast to the rich dark colours and strong patterns of the wallpaper. Only the domestic quarters of the better houses and of the really poor were, by now, colour washed (as has been observed when examining houses during

FIG. 269   *Burton Constable stage scenery c.1845, possibly by William Binks of Hull.*

demolition). The earlier records of Messrs. Cowtan the London wallpaper manufacturers, show that they shipped many orders by the Hull packet. The painted simulation of more expensive materials also included dummy windows painted as if half open as at 17 Pier Street (*fig*. 212)[88] and at Park Place, Park Street (c.1846, demolished 1978) where every alternat e first floor window had half open Venetian blinds correct in every detail painted in *trompe l'oeil* on the plaster box behind the fully glazed dummy windows. (The house at the northern end still retained its full complement of real and dummy blinds until the moment of demolition.) This group also had splendidly carved chimney-pieces of statuary marble with Greek Corinthian capitals and incised pilasters, as well as rich cornices whose choice of motifs alluded to the usage of the room — bold vines for the dining room that overlooked the terrace and the rear garden, and a band of garden flowers (roses, tulips, auriculas, narcissi, etc.) for the drawing room at the front of the house. In earlier days such decoration would have served as friezes, now they were fixed to the ceiling (which, to achieve some ventilation from the fumes of gas lighting, was noticeably higher than in the 18th century). Staircases had either wooden or iron balusters, the former turned, with a vertically symmetrical pattern of mouldings as in the Park Street area (*fig*. 272), the latter much more richly decorated with leaves, knops, anthemion and other classical motifs. The smooth upward curving handrail remained the most popular form, with, in addition, curving steps at the foot of the stairs in the French manner, and an apse at the half landing (*fig*. 273). Some houses had side board recesses (*fig*. 57), a good example surviving at 2 Baker Street. In the suburbs most builders sought to link house and garden either by inserting a pair of wide glazed doors between them, or by an ingenious triple sash window that allowed the bottommost to be lowered into a pit below floor level, so that the occupants of the room could walk outside without difficulty. By the 1830's the corner pieces of the windows were in brightly coloured glass, blue, green, red or yellow.[89]

FIG. 270 (opposite, above left) *Park Street, porch by William Foale, architect, c.1845, demolished 1978.* FIG. 271 (opposite, above right) *Entrance hall.* FIG. 272 (opposite bottom left) *Park Street (Nelson Terrace) detail of staircase.* FIG. 273 (opposite, bottom right) *Detail of* fig. 271. FIGS. 274 (above left), 275 (above right), 276 (bottom left), 277 (bottom right) *Park Street, details of dining and drawing room plasterwork of house* shown in fig. 270, *c.1845.*

FIG. 278 (opposite, above left) *Humber Place, c.1850.* FIG. 279 (opposite, above right) *Detail of doorcase.* FIG. 280 (opposite, below) *Humber Dock entrance to lock, c.1846 (Minerva Terrace in background).* FIG. 281 (above) *Warehouse from Humber Dock, J. B. Hartley, engineer-architect, 1845-46.* FIG. 282 (bottom) *Interior detail (see also fig. 192).*

FIG. 283   *215 Anlaby Road, perhaps by George Jackson, c.1840-45.*

The growing number of gardens attached to the house meant a rapid decline in the number of separate garden plots that had, for example, been such a feature of Anlaby Road. On the 1855 Ordnance Map they were still prominent, but with the accelerating outward growth of Victorian Hull they were doomed to become building ground, thus severing a minor link between a common practice in Hull and on the continent.

Within the Old Town there was a comparative decline of High Street, old mansions became offices, or were demolished, and their sites covered by warehouses. Sheahan for example records the sale of 42, 43, High Street in 1828 and the building of the present warehouse (*fig.* 173) and the embedding of the remnant of the Crowle House in an office and warehouse block of 1849. The latter is essentially Georgian in style and if the window area is a little greater than one might expect, the same is equally true of Colonial Chambers, Princes Dock Side (*fig.* 195), specifically built as an office block in 1846, by Trinity House, to the designs of the surveyor, William Foale.

The opening of the Humber and Junction (now Princes) Docks in 1809 and 1829 respectively were followed by a spate of new buildings around the docks and piers, for the new paddle steamers did a substantial passenger as well as cargo trade for a time after the opening of the Hull and Selby railway in 1840 (*fig.* 131). In consequence there were plans for ranges of shops as well as offices and houses on the dockside, and houses such as 6-8 Pier Street (*fig.* 208) (built for Edward Rheam, currier, in 1824, dem.1978)[90] had the ground floor rooms occupied as shipping offices, the first floor as reception rooms, the kitchen and bedrooms on the second floor and further bedrooms on the top storey. Of the many trade cards long hidden behind an office chimney-piece one announced the sailing times on 13th May, 1844, for Bremen, of the iron archimedean screw steam vessel 'Margaret' (one of the pioneer screw vessels built by Pims of English Street Works, 1843), others depicted the small coaches and trucks used on the contemporary railways, and it was in fact the latter which were soon to contribute to the dwindling prosperity of the Old Town, in particular when Paragon Station opened in 1846. (For some time J. B. Hartley's handsome warehouse did duty as a passenger terminal for those who arrived by sea.) (*Figs.* 281, 282.) By 1850 few among the fashionable cared to live within the ring of docks. The coming of the railway did however so reduce the transport time and cost of bringing good building stone into Hull that architects were encouraged to use it generously. For most this meant continuing in the classical idiom, building with the porticoes and bold cornices that the early Victorians readily accepted in stone but which they felt were something of a sham, if in painted stucco. Hence something of the Georgian era continued to tinge the architecture of Victorian Hull (*figs.* 267 a-b). The new mood can be sensed in the fine front of Dr. James Alderson's house in Albion Street (c.1846) (*fig.* 69), but a deeper study of Victorian Hull must wait for publication.

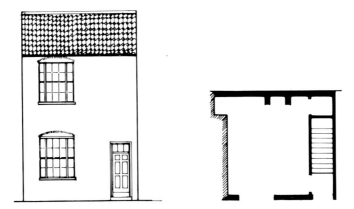

Fig. 284   *Courtyard house behind George Street, Riddells, builders, c.1792.*

Notes

THE ENTRIES IN THE BENCH BOOK of the Hull Municipal Corporation and the Vote Books of Trinity House are given here only by calendar date. The Memorials in the Land Registry are given as volume number and page number.

The reference to the histories of Hull are recorded by the author's surnames, viz:

Hadley — George Hadley — *History of Kingston-upon-Hull* 1788

Tickell — John Tickell — *History of Hull* 1796

Sheahan — J. J. Sheahan — *History of Hull* 1864

Greenwood — *Picture of Hull* 1835

For a select bibliography see Dr. Gordon Jackson's *Hull in the Eighteenth Century,* p. 438 and the *History of the County of York, East Riding,* Vol. I, 1969, *The Victoria County History of Hull.*

Collections of Yorkshire prints and drawings outside Hull are in the Gott Collection, Wakefield Art Gallery and the Hailstone Collection, York Minster Library.

ABBREVIATIONS

City R.O. — Hull City Records Office
H.C.R.O. — Humberside Record Office
H.U.L. — Hull University Library
R.D. — Registry of Deeds – H.C.R.O.

T.H. — Trinity House
W.H. — Wilberforce House
B.B. — Bench Book, City R.O.
V.C.H. — Victoria County History

INTRODUCTION

1 See frontispiece of V.C.H.
2 For a general review of the history of Hull, see op. cit. above.
3 Both Jeremiah Hargrave and T. W. Wallis did ship carving.

17TH CENTURY

4 Information obtained at the Chapel Lane Staithe excavation, 1978.
5 V.C.H., p. 132
6 Op. cit., p. 133.
7 The history of the cross is given in B.B., eg. 1680, p. 126; 1682, p. 736; etc. Is the Richard Roebuck mentioned the same as was working in Beverley Minster 1719 and 1725 (also in marble) and in 1717 at St. Mary's, Lowgate?
8 B.B. 1682, p. 705.
9 B.B. 1682, p. 765.
10 B.B. 1682, p. 173.
11 Messrs. Littlewoods now occupy the site.

THE DEVELOPERS

12 Sheahan, pp. 391-406.
13 Deeds held by present owner of the property.
14 R.D. AD187
15 R.D. Z245 and BD20
16 H.C.R.O. DDGR 42/41 and B.B. 1771
17 Battle's Directory 1791 and 1803
18 R.D. AU3/3 AU6/3.
19 Messrs. Hammond and Riddell's contract was for £734 3s. 9d. (*The History of Fish Street Church, Hull,* 1899).

20 H.C.R.O. DDHB 29/81 and 92.
21 H.C.R.O. DDHB 20/7-13, 170-213
22 H.C.R.O. DDHB 20/177 A note on the back states 'late in the occupation of William Ringrose (a builder) sold to William Lee'.
23 For land prices between 1771 and 1788, see H.C.R.O. DDHB57/4. For Pycock's transaction R.D. BT497.
24 R.D. BH7 & Hull Rental 1798 (City R.O.)
25 R.D. BC530 and BH274.
26 R.D. U369.
27 City R.O. TLA19
28 City R.O. BRD describes conditions for building. At auction £5 5s. 0d. per yard was paid for Queen Street frontage, £1 6s. 0d. per sq. yard in passage.
29 City R.O. drawings.
30 Gott Collection, Wakefield, contains one copy.
31 H.R.C.O. DDGR 42/14 et al. See E. Ingram *Leaves of a family tree* for an account of the Grimston/Maister correspondence. R.D. BL309.
32 E.g. R.D. BS389 and 373 and BQ212. For House plan R.D. Vol. 178, p. 55, 1917.
33 Information from A. G. Chamberlain.
34 V.C.H., p. 449. City R.O. TLA 34587 and H.C.R.O. DDHB 20/112. Land prices for 1781 c.7/3d. per sq. yard for Savile Street, George Street c.6/4d., Charlotte Street c.4/10d.
35 R.D. CF521 describes the garden 'formerly a complete oval'.
36 E.g. City R.O. TLA 34587. Pease 'sold' to the builders, Fox and Usher, without a conveyance.
37 Pease account books (to be moved to City R.O.).
38 R.D. BL557.
39 Tickell, pp. 849-50.
40 R.D. CL194

41 R.D. EL391 Appleton Bennison's will — leaves two houses in York Street, having bought one and garden in 1811.
42 *Hull Advertiser,* Aug. 23rd, 1800. *Hull Advertiser,* Sept. 29th, 1804. A sale notice describes a gallery over the bow window for viewing ships
43 *Hull Advertiser,* Sept. 13th, 1822 advertises houses on a new plan 'uniting the advantages of Town and Country'.
44 A plan of Myton (City R.O. CH944) c.1810 shows the pattern of building development as well as landowners' names.
   H.C.R.O. DDHB 29/7.
   Hull Advertiser, July 3rd, 1802. Advertisement for contractors describes the intended Chapel, Paragon and South Streets.

MID-GEORGIAN

45 Isaac Ware, *A Complete Body of Architecture.*
46 Ware, op. cit.
47 William Kent, *Designs of Inigo Jones,* London, 1727, pl. 55.
48 H.U.L. Maister letters, Nov. 7th, 1744.
49 Pl. 89, Vol. II.
50 Isaac Ware, *Designs of Inigo Jones,* pl. 34.
51 Rebuilt by S. Spencer, 1744 (H.U.L. Maister letters).
52 R.D. Z170 & D.D. HB57/4.
53 A similar but now restored terrace is at 9-13 Bishop Lane. R.D. Z226 and City R.O. Hull Rental 1798.
54 R.D. U410.
55 Isaac Ware, *A Complete Body of Architecture.*
56 Edward Ingram, *Transactions of the Georgian Soc. for E. Yorks,* Vol. IV, pt. II and *Our Lady of Hull* (1948).

CRAFTSMEN

57 *Hull Packet,* July 21st, 1795.
58 Information obtained from Trinity House rent rolls and H.C.R.O. DDCC vouchers and DDHA 14/27 a letter from Hargrave to Lord Langdale's steward.
59 *Country Life,* June 3rd, 1976, p. 1476. I. Hall discusses Constable's relationship with his craftsmen.
60 Portland Papers, DWF3.956.
61 *Hull Packet,* Dec. 30th, 1794.
62 I. Hall, *William Constable as patron.* Ferens Art Gallery, Hull, 1970.
63 H.R.C.O. DDCC Vouchers, Aug. 29th, 1777. The glasses cost £243 6s. 0d.
64 As above, Dec. 2nd, 1784.
65 Thomas Wilkinson Wallis — *Autobiography* — Louth 1899, p. 35, 'outside at some ship-carvers in Gibson's shipyard, designing the patterns as I went on'.
66 See trade card as found on palm tree corner stand, *fig.* 104.
67 H.C.R.O. DDCC Vouchers, Oct., 1841.

68 As above, June 12th, 1841.
69 *Transactions of the Georgian Society for East Yorks.,* Vol. III, Part I, p. 27.

TRINITY HOUSE

70 T.H. Letter Book, Sept. 5th, 1737. Vote Book, Aug. 23rd, 1737.
71 Names derived from the rentals.
72 T.H. Vote Book, April 3rd, 1764. Much of the subsequent information is also taken from the Vote Books.
73 *Hull Advertiser,* July 1st, 1800
74 T.H. Vote Book, April 18th, 1789.
75 T.H. Letter Book, July 21st, 1772 et. al., reveal the extent of Chambers work for Trinity House.
76 T.H. Vote Book. On July 31st, 1773, Page was paid 6 guineas for plans and elevations for improving the Council Room and Ladies Room.
77 T.H. Account Book. Lockwood was paid £40 for plans Aug. 5th, 1840.
78 T.H. Vote Book, May 7th, 1842. William Foale appointed Surveyor.

ADAM

79 Newcastle Art Gallery, Bewick Day Books show costs of 18s. 0d. and 5s. 0d. respectively, also c.f. Hadley Arms & Seals, opp. p. 702 for design.
80 The earliest mahogany doors are probably those at Haworth Hall, later examples in Charlotte Street had panels edged with finely figured crossbanding on the showy side but with dummy joints in the appropriate positions on the other.
81 City R.O. 1739-1826, Charterhouse accounts.
82 Now installed at Central Cottage, Lastingham.
83 Boulton and Watt papers, Birmingham Reference Library Folio 29. For date erected and rateable value, see Sculcoates Rate Books, 1787-95.
84 *Hull Packet,* July 21st, 1795.
85 Collection at Hull Museum.

REGENCY

86 Gott Collection at Wakefield City Art Gallery.
87 Drawing in the Burton Constable Collection.
88 Built for William Westerdale, block and tackle maker, c.1817.
89 A good example is at 97 Spring Bank, c.1841 for Henry Handsom.
90 R.D. DU10
91 City R.O. TLA 29600 records the rebuilding of the property from a coach house, 1802.
92 The only surviving Georgian house in the northern section of Grimston Close, built up c.1829 on soil from the dock.

Index

Page references in light type. Figure references in bold type.